PENGUIN BOOKS

YOU CAN MAKE YOUR DREAMS WORK

Shalini Umachandran is a journalist with the *Times of India*. She has previously worked for *The Hindu* and the *Economic Times*, and has covered a range of topics from travel and the arts to environment and politics. This is her first book.

Find more stories of switching careers at www.shaliniumachandran.com.

YOU CAN MAKE YOUR DREAMS WORK

INSPIRATIONAL STORIES OF 15 INNOVATORS

SHALINI UMACHANDRAN

PENGUIN BOOKS

An imprint of Penguin Random House

PENGUIN BOOKS

USA | Canada | UK | Ireland | Australia
New Zealand | India | South Africa | China | Singapore

Penguin Books is part of the Penguin Random House group of companies
whose addresses can be found at global.penguinrandomhouse.com

Published by Penguin Random House India Pvt. Ltd
4th Floor, Capital Tower 1, MG Road,
Gurugram 122 002, Haryana, India

Penguin
Random House
India

First published by Penguin Books India 2015

10 9 8 7 6 5 4 3 2

ISBN 9780143418535

Typeset in Minion Pro by Manipal Digital Systems, Manipal
Printed at Repro India Limited

www.penguin.co.in

For my parents,
Prema and Umachandran.
Thank you for holding me close while letting go.
All that I am is because of you.

Contents

INTRODUCTION

When I was in my twenties, all I wanted to do was open a bookstore. I planned it, dreamt about it, talked about it, and took a year off from journalism to learn the book business, but I never got around to doing it because I was unsure of whether I *would* be able to make a go of it.

The upside of that year away was that I realized I loved to write about and tell stories of real people as much as I loved the idea of being surrounded by books all day. If I hadn't taken that break, if I had been too afraid to leave the stability of a newspaper job, I would never have come around to that realization. Since then, I've always been intrigued by people who let go to seek happiness that isn't linked only to money and success.

The first person I know who abandoned one career in favour of another is my friend and former colleague Prassana Srinivasan. Prassana had always wanted to teach, but had been discouraged by the pay, which was worse than a journalist's. She finally quit, and enrolled in a Montessori teacher-training course. She was scared. She wasn't earning much. But she loved it, and when she finally had a class of her own, she was convinced it was worth it.

A trip to Ladakh a few years ago got me thinking about career switches again. Before we set off on the gruelling but beautiful two-day drive up to Leh, we spent a couple of days at a guest house in Manali, which was run by a former colleague of a friend. Nishant Singh had abandoned an eight-year corporate career to follow his dream of being in the hospitality business in the mountains.

What does it take to do that, I wondered. To be so driven by an idea or a passion that one leaves a career built on years of hard work and goes all out to set a new course. I wanted to understand *how* one confronted an all-consuming passion and made the switch.

'Find out,' said Kamini Mahadevan, who went on to become my editor, when we met for coffee one day and the conversation veered to career changes. 'And write about it.'

And so began the hunt for people who had switched careers to do what they love. I called and emailed friends and friends of friends, scoured the Internet and read anything that had the words 'career' and 'change' in it, and drew up a list of more than 100 people who had taken a second shot at their professional lives.

Once I started my research for this book, I was amazed by the number of people who wanted to share their stories. Some of them gave me fantastic leads, some told me their stories, some wanted to hear about the stories I was finding because they hadn't been able to take that plunge or they didn't know where their passion lay. Others just wanted to talk about how they had found a passion that became an all-consuming hobby and kept them going at their day jobs.

I drew up a list of more than 100 people who felt their lives needed something more, and so quit and changed track. I had long phone conversations with most of them and shortlisted and met about thirty people who left successful or promising corporate careers, because they had an idea or a dream that, quite literally, did not let them sleep.

I've picked people who threw everything in, who took an all-or-nothing chance to live a life that gave them a sense of purpose. The final fifteen in these pages are people like you and me, people you probably know; they're not famous, they're not billionaires. They made the switch without knowing what would happen, trusting only in their instincts and self-belief, often going against conventional wisdom and counsel from parents, friends and employers. The pure desire for entrepreneurship alone was not enough; I chose people for whom the new career was almost a calling. The thread that runs through these stories is a desire to find a purpose in life and realizing that money and society's measures of success alone are not enough.

For these fifteen, success is about being able to work by their own rules, and set and keep moving the goalposts. Their motivation is achieving a high quality of life, and they consciously decide what it is that they want from a career. In this book, they share that process of decision-making, the struggle of staying the new course and their tips for making the switch.

Quite a few people dream of a different life. In the newsroom where I work, it's fairly common to find aspiring actors, artists, directors, writers and musicians earning their keep till they get their big break. Following a dream is a tempting whim that most of us don't act on, because circumstances don't allow us to, because we don't have the courage to follow through, because we're waiting for the perfect time, or because we're not really sure what we want to do. They're the same kind of doubts that each person in this book faced up to and decided to stop analysing and start doing.

And they discovered that they're so much happier for having done what they set out to do.

PLAYING THE FIELD

Rohit Singal

Rohit Singal spent ten years as a doctor before giving in to his real love, information technology. He set up Sourcebits, one of the first Indian companies to build products for Apple. Ten years later, he sold the company in a multimillion-dollar deal, and now, as founder of mobile gaming studio Wandake, plays games for a living.

There's a spartan elegance to Rohit Singal's office in Bangalore's Electronic City; it's simple and stylish, yet every element is rooted in function—a lot like the applications his company builds. Two Apple monitors dominate the clutter-free desk set in one side of the room. He conducts meetings at a high, polished square table, and flops down to think on a white floor-cushion in another corner. The only incongruity in the organic space is the abundance of artificial flowers.

1

'In this environment, you can't have real plants,' says Rohit, a bright-eyed thirty-eight-year-old, in a deadpan voice that seems to make his Haryanvi-accented English seem blunter than it is. Fake flowers are lined up along a shelf above his desk with the two monitors, blossoming plastic squares sit at the centre of the meeting table, and larger palms along the massive sheet-glass windows look on to a real, flowering tree outside.

'I would have taken up some career in floriculture or horticulture, but in the 1990s you didn't have the option. I was the only boy in my neighbourhood interested in gardening when I was growing up in Haryana. It was considered a woman's field,' says Rohit, who raised a range of flowering plants, cacti and succulents and won a few state- and national-level awards for gardening in his hometown.

So he joined a medical college, but, during the ten years of studying and practising medicine, he realized that his real love was technology—something that provided him a creative outlet. He started the design-driven software company Sourcebits in 2006 to build mobile applications such as the popular Night Stand, which converts the iPhone into a clock and earned his company its first million within two years of operation. By July 2014, Sourcebits had grown to earn revenues of $8.5 million and was acquired by the London-headquartered mobile software services company Globo, leaving Rohit to focus entirely on his mobile gaming apps studio Wandake.

It was through gaming that Rohit discovered his love for technology while he was in Rohtak's government medical college. 'It was primarily my parents' wish that I study medicine. I was not mature enough to take my own decisions and they were so proud when I cleared the all-India test,' he says. 'We were a middle-class family and medicine was even shinier than engineering. So both my younger brother and I became doctors.' Rohit's wife, Pooja, is also a doctor.

Rohit's father, an engineer with the National Highways Authority of India, bought a computer when Rohit was in his third year of medical college. Rohit began tinkering with it—taking it apart and rebuilding and playing games like Diablo and Age of Empires. 'This was around 1996–97, when there was no Internet in Haryana, but I would experiment and modify to create new things,' he says. Rohit constantly doodles on an electronic slate, a Boogie Board, while he talks—drawing, scrawling words, underlining and boxing them, only to erase and do it over, starting with a new idea. It is this restless need to keep creating new things that drives Rohit. It is also the reason why he couldn't stick to the field of medicine.

'In medicine, there was no scope to do things differently, no need to analyse. Everything is documented and you have to follow set practices. Experimenting, in fact, can be very dangerous,' he says. As a child and as a gardener, Rohit had loved the idea of grafting—bringing together two varieties of plants to create a third, new one—and cross-pollination. Medicine, he realized to his dismay, gave him no opportunity to innovate.

After gardening, dabbling in technology seemed the only way to learn new things. 'I could create more by myself, whether [manipulating] an image in Photoshop, using an application to create a 3D object, or writing a solution. That excited me,' he says. 'I still love to try new things and it has made us stand apart. Eventually, when we started Sourcebits, we built programmes and applications that did not exist on the Apple platform. We were the first Indian company to do that.'

By the time he finished his MBBS degree in 2000, Rohit had discovered the Internet and knew that the emerging world of information technology was what he loved, but was diffident about telling his family that he wanted to abandon medicine. So he moved to Chennai to work with a leading cardiologist, but as the year passed, he became more convinced than ever that he didn't have the aptitude or the appropriate bedside manner to be a doctor. 'I don't think I am a person suitable to be a doctor and interact with patients. It requires a particular touch, which I did not have,' he says. 'I had found my passion in technology.'

In 2002, he moved to Bangalore to do an MD in radiology at M.S. Ramaiah Medical College, choosing the subject only because it used computers for diagnosis. He worked on a teleradiology project with a doctor from the University of Rochester and learnt to archive images. So when his college was looking for software to archive radiology images and scans for doctors, which could be recalled easily, Rohit knew exactly what kind of solution they needed. He customized an image archival and communication system using open-source software and sold it to the college with the help of his professor for $100,000. Siemens and other large organizations were quoting upwards of $1 million. Plus, Rohit agreed to receive the payments in monthly instalments of Rs 2 lakh over two years. 'Finally, I got to do something constructive in college,' he says with a cheeky grin.

Putting together the image archival software also introduced him to the iMac G3, Apple's flagship desktop, which turned the company's fortunes around in the late 1990s. 'I never went back to a PC after that,' says Rohit. 'The ease of use and beauty of the design had me hooked. I wanted to design like that.'

The initial success made Rohit surer of an escape from medicine after he finished his MD in October 2005. 'It gave me the confidence that someone would pay for my abilities, that maybe I could do something I enjoyed,' he says. The promise of a guaranteed pay-out from the college for the next two years added a sense of stability.

He quit and set up iPacx, a company to market the image archival software, but couldn't find a single buyer because no hospital used expensive Apple systems in the mid-2000s. Even finding people who knew how to work on the Mac platform was difficult. After three or four months, he had to face the fact that iPacx would not take off.

'I was really, really scared that I'd have to go back to medicine. That fear pushed me to think about building more products,' he says. The thought of adapting to the omnipresent Windows platform did not cross his mind— he enjoyed working on a Mac. He believed he just needed to build products that people were more likely to use. In April 2006 he set up Sourcebits with the idea of creating design-driven applications for the Mac system.

The launch of the iPhone was more than a year away; the iPad was only a prototype, and the Mac was prohibitively expensive for most Indians, but Rohit believed that software needed to be more intuitive and user-friendly. 'I could have stayed in radiology, where the starting salary is Rs 1.5 lakh a month. No headache, no real responsibility towards the patients . . . you work seven to eight hours a day. But I wanted to do something that I truly enjoyed, and Mac fit the bill at that point,' he says.

He was thirty when he rented Sourcebits's first office —a parking lot that had been converted into an office near his alma mater in Bangalore. 'I felt proud that I was finally doing something on my own. We were like every other

American start-up working in a garage, only I didn't know it then. The difference between us and them was that we paid rent for the garage, Rs 12,000 a month,' he says.

While his wife supported his decision, his father, G.R. Singal, was quite upset by the fact that his son had veered off course and tried to talk him out of it. 'I kept telling him it's going to be fine. He grumbled, but accepted [what I was saying] and would drop in at the office to see what we were up to. Maybe he thought I could try this for a couple of years and then go back,' Rohit says. 'I was very clear that this would be my life.' And for the next eight years, Sourcebits was his life.

The original plan was to create medical software that doctors could use without the help of technicians. Once he hired his first two employees, his ideas changed. 'I had never interacted with engineers or designers before. Once I did, my brain started thinking beyond medical applications,' he says.

Among those first employees was a medical college dropout, Hage Yaapa, who'd spent two years just hunkered down in his room, messing around on a computer and teaching himself how to design web pages and write basic code. 'I was not looking for any kind of expertise because I didn't have expertise,' says Rohit. 'I wanted to work with people like myself. I still hire people who are passionate about what they want to do, people who are looking for something different to do, people like me. My team inspires me.' Rohit insists that Yaapa, his second employee Jimmy Jacob and chief innovation officer Piotr Gajos (who joined Sourcebits in 2008 and finessed the design-led culture that Rohit set out to establish) be mentioned when any story of the company is being told.

Rohit met Yaapa after the guy who fixed their Internet connections introduced them. 'I dropped out of medical college after two years because I was crazy about design,' says Yaapa, who moved to Bangalore where all the IT buzz was in 2003. 'I'd been trying to do my own thing for two years. I decided to join Rohit because he seemed smart, not boring, and I liked the ideas he had,' says Yaapa, who is now Vice President, Products, at Sourcebits. 'When something interests him, he just goes crazy. I like and respect that. I had never seen a Mac before, but it didn't stop him from hiring me, and I learnt.' Rohit found his second employee, Jimmy, one of the few Mac programmers in the area, through online forums. Jimmy too is still with Sourcebits as a vice president.

The first application the tiny team built was Fun Booth, which allowed users to add masks, fake moustaches, hats and other props in real time to photos and videos taken with a webcam. They spent six months on development and it hit the market in November 2006. The focus was on design and user interface, hanging on a couple of lines of simple code—just the kind of simple elegance that the Mac community loved. At its peak, Fun Booth clocked about 5000 downloads a day and, close to a decade later, is still listed among the top-100 Apple apps.

'We didn't think: Who will use these products, who will buy, how will we make money? We just wanted to make them and thought someone like us would buy,' says Rohit, an admirer of Apple founder Steve Jobs's work style and ethic.

Fun Booth's popularity didn't bring in loads of money, but it earned them publicity and clients from the US looking for web-based solutions. 'Typically, Indian companies appoint sales people in the US and other geographies to bring in clients. In our case, we built apps that the Mac community noticed, so the clients came to us. That continues to be the case even today,' says Rohit, who counts GE, Intel, MIT, P&G, Hershey's, Coca-Cola, ESRI, Fossil and the US Military among Sourcebits's clients. 'I'm very proud of Fun Booth because it provided the confidence that we could conceptualize, build and ship a product that the world recognized.'

Yaapa remembers the day they got their first international client after Fun Booth was released. 'It was $20,000 for a web-based solution and we were so excited. We closed up the office and went to Brigade Road to celebrate,' says Yaapa. 'The energy was fantastic. I didn't know it was a start-up environment, but that's what we were a part of.'

Until then, says Rohit, he was scared. 'I will not say I had doubts. I would say I was fearful. I was fearful of things not working out and having to return to medicine. I don't know what I would have done if Sourcebits hadn't taken off, but fortunately it did.'

Over the next year, the garage got rather crowded as they grew to twenty people developing their own products as well as creating new ones for clients. Towards the end of 2008, a year after the first-generation iPhone was launched, Sourcebits launched Night Stand, an app that turned the mobile phone into a bedside clock. 'People had to spend $50 to $100 on a bedside clock. Here was a free app that did the job,' Rohit says.

Night Stand, one of the first iPhone apps in the world, was all about presentation and design, with just three or four lines of coding. 'Now, a clock app is a default on any phone, but back then we were the first to build it. Two to three million downloads happened in no time and all of a sudden we were bombarded with requests for different kinds of applications,' says Rohit. 'That was when we really started growing.' They opened a small sales office in Atlanta in the US, and by mid-2009 they could afford a proper office in Rajaji Nagar in Bangalore and hire seventy more employees. Sourcebits began to look like a real IT company.

Rohit is extremely proud of the fact that his company has always built for the international market under its own name. 'Apart from Tally, it is rare to find an Indian company building a software product for the international market that has become a hit. Many Indian companies work on the development of big products like Photoshop and Windows, but they are doing outsourcing work for other larger companies. They don't get credited individually for it. We were unique because we built and sold our own products under our own name. And we were successful doing it.'

Another large fish that Sourcebits landed was the contract to build Coca-Cola's very first mobile app, Coke Cheers, in 2009. 'When the app went live in January 2010, it was a big moment for me and one of the world's best-known brands.' In January 2010, Sourcebits moved to a 46,000-sq. ft office in the IT hub of Electronic City and soon had more than 100 employees.

Sourcebits stood apart because it focused on design in a country driven purely by engineering. Most entrepreneurs in the tech space have an engineering background, with little or no exposure to design, since college courses have no modules on user-interface design. Design school graduates rarely look for jobs in the tech world as it is considered geeky and boring. 'If you are making products for people, you have to get the user interaction right and then worry about the nuts-and-bolts engineering, which is not so difficult. Most apps don't need too much engineering, though you do need strength in some technical areas,' says Rohit, who hired a designer for about Rs 4 lakh a year, when Sourcebits's turnover was Rs 7 lakh. 'I just believed that was right for Sourcebits,' he says simply, when asked about a decision that is considered crazy in the market.

Decisions like these that seem to defy accepted business logic and constant experimentation are Rohit's fuel, and he's quick to accept that many of his radical ideas have failed, though a fair number have taken off too. In 2011, after it got $10 million in funding from Sequoia Capital and IDG Ventures, Sourcebits moved its headquarters to San Francisco, a savvy decision to draw the best talent and clients, but then went on to set up a suite of smaller offices across the US, which turned out to be more of a failure than a success.

'I come up with new ideas to keep myself and my team excited about work,' he says. 'We hit the headlines in India only after we got funding, though we were well established and profitable before that. So I suppose you can say money talks,' he says, laughing.

A gamble that didn't pay off so well was an experiment with a partnership model—each Sourcebits business unit would run as an individual entity, with the head as a partner. The unit would compete with other Sourcebits units as well as outside companies for clients. The metaphor for it would be a mall—you go there knowing you want to buy a pair of shoes, but you choose the brand once you're there, depending on how a particular store reels you in. Similarly, Sourcebits would be a platform that clients approached for technology development, but they would decide which unit they wanted to work with rather than the company deciding on the team. So each unit would have to, in a sense, pitch for the client. 'It was an exciting idea for me because we were trying to make Sourcebits itself the product. The idea was to make each unit small and nimble, so that the innovation and execution is really fast, which would have been radically different from the way any Indian company works. But it didn't work,' he shrugs. 'Mistakes help you learn and keep things interesting.'

Working with Rohit is described as a perpetual adventure. 'It's like flying an aeroplane with almost no fuel left. You're always on the edge, you think you can't go any further—which is when Rohit casually walks in and pushes you even harder,' says Piotr, who joined Sourcebits in 2008 as head of Interaction Design and was its first overseas employee.

In April 2014, Gartner, an American information technology research and advisory firm, named Sourcebits a 'Cool Vendor in Services', and in July, Rohit made the announcement that the company was being acquired by Globo and that he was leaving. 'Earlier in the year, I began considering the future of Sourcebits. Profits were considerable and growth was 100 per cent year-on-year, but I wanted a change. It was a hard decision, like leaving my home, my child, but, ultimately, if I wanted to keep life interesting, exciting, follow my heart, I needed to leave,' he says. At the time of his exit, Sourcebits had about 250 employees, more than 150 of them in the US, and had developed more than 500 applications for multiple mobile, web and desktop platforms.

Wandake, Japanese for 'only one', is Rohit's new toy. The studio has built popular games such as Robokill, which Rohit describes as his favourite product, and Apocalypse. 'Building my own products through Wandake is a higher risk proposition, but it's going to be more fun,' he says. 'So, you see, I do not come to work, this is my playground.'

ROHIT'S ADVICE

1. Don't build up challenges in your head. When you use the word 'challenge', it's mostly your brain telling you that this thing is quite difficult and needs a lot of effort, so it's better not to do it. If you are more passionate about another field and want to leave your current job, do it. Do not wait.
2. Find a team as passionate as you are about the work you are doing, so that you inspire one another. Surround yourself and your team with the magic word 'yes'.
3. Do not be afraid of mistakes. I make mistakes every week. I love them because I learn from them.

HIS OWN ANNAPURNA

Dinesh K.S.

His great love for the outdoors prompted Dinesh K.S. to abandon his engineering job and head out to climb rocks and mountains. But after an accident put a stop to his adventures, he turned his attention to the lack of affordable, good-quality trekking equipment in India. The company he started in a garage in the early 1990s, Wildcraft, is on track to become a Rs 500-crore brand by 2017–18.

Dinesh K.S. was twenty when he first read *Annapurna*, a book by French mountaineer Maurice Herzog that details a rather reckless yet valiant first expedition in 1950 to scale the 8091-m mountain in the Himalayas. It's a rather grandiose, one-sided account of the ascent of a challenging peak, which demanded far more than just courage from its climbers—Herzog and fellow climber Louis Lachenal lost fingers and toes to frostbite and the price of victory was that neither could climb quite as well ever again.

Annapurna is one of the many books on exploration and mountaineering that inspired Dinesh, the founder of outdoor apparel and gear company Wildcraft, to take up mountain climbing and trekking, a lifelong love that would influence the business he went on to set up in 1993. He would continue to nurture and labour over the company as it touched Rs 100 crore in 2013. In many ways, Wildcraft has been Dinesh's own Annapurna, demanding of him more than he wanted to give, bestowing a sense of achievement, sending him into absolute lows, teaching him valuable lessons and endowing him with the prescience to spot danger and avoid risk.

Dinesh set off on his first trip to the Himalayas in 1982, driven by a desire to see and experience all he had read about in books by early twentieth-century European explorers such as Eric Shipton, Herzog and Reinhold Messner. 'Those books captivated me. The drive, the pride, the passion those Europeans had for the mountains had me hooked,' says Dinesh, who was born in 1961.

Dinesh was a student of electronic engineering at Bangalore University, a course he'd chosen as a safe option as he didn't know where his real interest lay. In the library, though, he discovered a love for the outdoors. 'The adventures those people wrote about were gripping. I wanted to see those places, feel that sense of excitement and discovery, overcome challenges and reach goals I set for myself, just like they had,' he says.

The trip to Nepal exceeded all his expectations. 'After that trip, I lost all interest in engineering. I was hooked to adventure sports and I started trekking and climbing as much as I could around Bangalore. Being outdoors made me focus, connect with myself and feel like I was living every moment,' he says. He loved the physical sensation of moving upwards on rock, the sense of solitude that came with being so close to nature, and the camaraderie one shared with the trekking team. 'A transformation was taking place; realization was guiding me and it cemented in me a belief: There is happiness in simplicity.'

'Unfortunately, there was no hope of making a living out of these things in the 1980s. Even getting a job was difficult in those days unless you were from a prestigious institute like an IIT,' says Dinesh, who finished his course in 1985. 'And I didn't have the best marks.'

Before he started work at a television company in Bangalore in 1986, he gave himself the gift of a month-long course at the Himalayan Mountaineering Institute in Darjeeling. 'It was the only way to spend a month in the mountains for just Rs 600. Plus, it seemed like the logical step for someone who wanted to be outdoors all the time. Then I came back to Bangalore, buckled down and worked,' he says. The weekend trips near Bangalore continued, but there was no time to go farther afield.

After spending a couple of years as an office drone, Dinesh planned an expedition to the Bandarpunch peak located in the Garhwal Himalayas in Uttarakhand with a few friends. He made all the arrangements and then realized to his horror that he would not get time off because the 1988 Seoul Olympics was around the corner and the company needed all hands on deck. 'I didn't get leave, so I quit. I'm not sure what I was thinking when I resigned, I just did. I wanted to go on the trip—it meant more to me than the job,' he says.

It had been close to two years since he had been to the Himalayas and the completeness he felt during the expedition only increased his love for the mountains. He loved the idea of pushing himself to scale a peak, the feeling of being part of a team and working together towards a goal, and the sheer beauty of nature. The following year Dinesh met a climber and adventure-sports instructor who told him about the National Outdoor Leadership School (NOLS) in the US, where he had trained. 'It sounded perfect to me—earning a living by going up into the mountains.'

Back in Bangalore, Dinesh began the process of applying for the instructor course at NOLS. 'I got accepted with a complete scholarship, and was all set to leave in May 1990, when I met with an accident and broke my ankle,' he says. Doctors debated whether he would ever be able to go trekking again, let alone climb mountains. 'It was a thought I could not bear.'

Instead of giving up on mountaineering entirely, he thought about what he could do to encourage more people to head outdoors. 'If I had to contemplate the idea of never being able to climb again, I at least wanted to share the joy I had felt with others around me and help them experience that feeling,' he says.

To cope with the long, slow process of recovery, he turned his head to making an aspiring climber's life easier. One of the main hurdles to climbing in India was the lack of proper climbing equipment. Most trekkers had to buy their gear from second-hand markets in Kathmandu or from Europe or the United States. During his trips to Nepal, Dinesh would scour the second-hand markets for rucksacks, tents, ropes, carabiners, boots and all the other equipment he needed, and would bring back extras for his friends. European and American climbers rarely took back all the equipment they brought along on expeditions, so the lanes of Kathmandu were filled with best-quality trekking and mountaineering gear. 'The only problem was that we had to go all the way north and across the border every time we needed something, and then struggle to get it through customs. Not at all practical.' In January 1991, Dinesh decided to make the kind of gear he and his friends liked to use, so that expeditions into the wild would be simpler and less expensive.

'If you have a passion for a sport, you also have a love for the equipment used for the sport. It is so important for people to have good equipment; it can be as basic as a backpack, which is what we sell most, but it makes such a difference. I knew what was lacking here in India. So I said, let's fill this blank,' he recalls.

Designing the equipment came easily to him since he had used the world's best gear. He also understood what a climber's needs were, what features were needed and which parts of the equipment took the most strain. 'To this day, we test our outdoor products ourselves by carrying the packs and using them. Using a product is the best way for you to learn to design it properly,' he says. 'It's something I keep telling the design team here.'

This was the era when 'bag' meant something to be carried on a train and so Dinesh didn't have any competition. 'There was no Internet, so I didn't know what the demand for this product was. I just started making it because I wanted to,' he says. 'Looking back, it was a very naive idea to make outdoor gear for a country that didn't have a culture of camping or trekking,' he says, breaking into his warm, full-throated laugh. Dinesh has a head of grey hair, a grey beard and the no-nonsense attitude of someone who has little sympathy for prevarication or dawdling.

One of the first products he made, after numerous visits to fabric suppliers and defence stockists, was a free-standing dome tent. 'I was the first to fabricate it in India, though it's not particularly hard to make. I made tents with material from a defence supplier and, along with a friend, took them to Zanskar in Ladakh and tested them,' he says. He booked a stall at a mountaineering trade show and displayed his used tents, which drew a lot of interest. 'But when I got down to making them, I realized there was a very small market, and it would be too expensive for individuals.'

He shifted his focus to backpacks, which had a market among weekend trekkers, and registered Wildcraft as a partnership firm in 1993, with two friends. 'We worked out of a garage in Jayanagar, Bangalore, which belonged to the father of one of the partners. I was the only one working full-time because the others had their own careers. I would go to the market for raw material, meet tailors and fabricators, and also try to sell the backpacks.'

The information technology sector was just taking off in Bangalore in the early 1990s, and companies looking to mimic a global work culture were organizing outdoor team activities. Weekend trekkers also included people who had returned from the US, where they had been introduced to camping and climbing. Word soon spread that there was a garage in Jayanagar where you could buy good-quality backpacks for a weekend in the wild as well as get information about the best destinations and meet like-minded adventure-lovers.

'From the 1980s, I had been exposed to world-class products, so I set very high standards from the beginning, ignoring existing practices in the industry. I sourced material for solid products, because when you talk of adventure, you cannot compromise on quality and reliability,' says Dinesh. 'Some of the early buyers still use those packs made in the 1990s.'

Till 1998, Wildcraft was essentially a one-man show. Dinesh used the front of the garage as his design room; the finished products were hung on hooks for sale along the back wall. On finalizing designs, Dinesh would head to the market on his motorbike to pick up the thread, straps, zips, buckles and other items, load them into two backpacks and ride to a factory in the Peenya industrial area, about 20 km away, where a friend let him use his sewing machines. 'He only charged me a basic amount for labour. He didn't charge for the space, lighting, electricity, use of machines. He was very generous, and that helped me get Wildcraft off the ground,' says Dinesh, who eventually had to train the tailors as the unit made shoes for the European market, not bags.

Two years on, Dinesh realized that the material he was using was not made locally. The supplier in Mumbai had run out of it and wasn't willing to bring in more. An outdoor product has to be light, durable, weather-resilient and affordable, which means that the kind of fabric used for both the inside and outside of the product is extremely important. 'We could not compromise and what we needed was not made locally. So we started importing fabric from Korea, though it was more expensive,' he says. 'We set a lot of trends in the industry. We've been importing fabric for twenty years now. We set such high standards from the beginning that the rest of the market had to catch up. Even today, we don't have any real domestic competition in the outdoor- and adventure-gear market,' he says.

In 1998, Wildcraft was registered as a private limited company and it appointed its first distributor. That's when Dinesh found that his pricing was wrong—after giving the distributor and dealers their margins, there wasn't much left for the company. Volumes were small and costs were high. The next year, the company moved from the Peenya factory to a house in Uttarahalli and bought a few of their own machines. By this time, Dinesh's ankle had healed completely and he was trekking and climbing again.

To promote its products and the outdoor culture, Wildcraft started running rafting and trekking camps near Bangalore and the Dandeli river. 'I thought people would learn to love nature and the outdoors through such activities, but that didn't happen. For young urban professionals, it was just an instant thrill, one more thing to tick off the list. Adventure sports catching on doesn't necessarily mean people are learning to love nature,' he says.

By 2000, Dinesh was quite heartsick—he hadn't been to the Himalayas since 1992 because Wildcraft consumed his every waking minute; the business wasn't really growing though the goodwill for the brand was tremendous; and his partners wanted to do things differently. 'We were just sustaining ourselves and there was a lot of uncertainty,' he says. 'By 2000, I had sort of given up and lost hope that Wildcraft would ever sustain me. I had been struggling for almost ten years and it was all hand to mouth. I was demoralized.'

Dinesh decided to stop and think instead of just pushing on, a lesson learnt from his climbing days. 'Any adventure sport involves an element of risk, and it's the same with business. You mitigate risk while climbing based on your skill, experience and equipment,' he says. 'That same ability to assess risk and the tools at your disposal help in business,' he says.

At thirty-nine, Dinesh had built a brand that was known for its quality and reliability; it was the first of its kind in India and he had won the goodwill of customers.

But he did not have the means to scale up, and there were loans and overdrafts to be paid. 'It seemed like there was not much I could contribute at that time. I decided to take a break, leave it to my partners and go back to my mountaineering, which I had neglected for years.' He picked up his dream of joining NOLS and moved to the US in April 2000 to do the instructor's course he had chosen ten years earlier.

'I spent three years at NOLS as a climbing instructor after I finished the course. I went to all the wild places most Americans have not seen. It was wonderful. Those years were just brilliant,' says Dinesh, his voice mellowing with memories of what clearly was one of the happiest times of his life. He spent about four days a month in a city and the rest in the backwoods and mountains of the Cascades from Arizona to California, with groups of eager students who loved nature like he did. He also taught courses that were conducted by NOLS in India.

During a holiday in Bangalore in July 2003, Dinesh got into a road accident and shattered his other ankle, effectively ending his career in the US as a climbing instructor. 'Indian roads are more dangerous than the mountains,' he says with a laugh, but quickly turns pensive. 'I am not sure that I would have come back if I had not met with an accident in mid-2003. It's very strange—fate kept me from going away to the school in the US in the 1990s because of which I started this. Everything turned upside down and I left it behind, but the second accident threw me back into this. I have thought about it many times,' he trails off and falls silent for a while.

While he had been away, a young MBA graduate had met Dinesh's partners while doing market research on the soft-luggage segment. Gaurav Dublish saw an opportunity for growth in the cash-strapped adventure-gear company; he, along with his friend from business school, Siddharth Sood, bought a stake in it with their savings, and brought his father on board as a director in 2001.

Siddharth and Gaurav had met at business school in Mumbai and hit it off from the start, drawn together by similar interests and a desire to be entrepreneurs, though they didn't have an idea of what sector they wanted to enter. After college, Gaurav joined the marketing team of luggage brand VIP and Siddharth joined GE's finance department. 'We both always wanted to be entrepreneurs, but didn't want to miss out on working for big brands,' says Gaurav, who is in his mid-thirties. 'I felt there was something Sid and I could do with Wildcraft at some point in the future, but just then our growth and learning curve in the corporate world was on the ascent. So we decided to put in some money and wait and see.'

In 2003 after Dinesh returned to India and was convalescing, he would hobble across to the factory, which had been moved out of Uttarahalli to Mysore Road. Soon enough, he realized that the company was not progressing at the rate it should be. 'I realized that if I wanted to save my baby, I must step in. The brand still enjoyed hard-won customer goodwill, and I knew what direction Wildcraft needed to take. I had worked too hard and given up too much to let it go. The break had given me that perspective.'

Gaurav and Siddharth gave carte blanche to Dinesh to get the company back on track. In 2004, one of the old partners turned over his shares while the other stayed away, and Dinesh started turning Wildcraft around. The first thing he did was move the factory back to Uttarahalli, where most of the staff lived. 'We had been spending lakhs every month transporting people from Uttarahalli to the factory,' says Dinesh.

In 2004, Gaurav suggested that they exit services—rafting camps and climbing activities—and focus on products, which they were known for, to consolidate the brand. 'I was quite hands-off till 2007 and would just check how things were going with Gaurav,' says Siddharth. 'Gaurav was my best friend and I liked and trusted Dinesh. I left it to them because I had my job and lived abroad.'

To expand and increase revenues without having to invest, Wildcraft decided to give out store franchises in 2004. The first three franchises were given to Dinesh's friends who had a love for the outdoors, money to invest and the business sense to keep the stores running. 'I got friends involved because I wanted people who understood the sport and the equipment. See, education is very important in our category; it's a niche segment and often the customer is looking for guidance. Why is one pack more expensive than the other, which is better, will it work in X conditions, do I need this?—these are the frequently asked questions that you need to answer. That's why I took on people who were familiar with the outdoors. With systems evolving and the huge scale of operations, we don't follow that any more,' he says. Wildcraft now retails from more than 120 exclusive stores in fifty cities, and has 2500 multi-brand stores in over 200 cities.

Though they had three successful franchise outlets and one company-owned store by 2006 and had touched Rs 2 crore in revenue, Dinesh knew he had done as much as he could for Wildcraft. 'In 2007, I called Gaurav and Siddharth and said, "This is where we are, and I have limitations.

I am a technical guy. We need a strategic plan; even though
we are good, if this company needs to go anywhere, we
need people like you from business schools with expertise
in marketing and finance,'" says Dinesh, and digresses to a
lesson from the outdoors.

While climbing Annapurna, Herzog had pushed ahead
though the weather conditions screamed hasty descent—
against the advice of all team members, including his
climbing partner, Lachenal. The team was carrying the
wrong gear—light boots for summer climbing, but too
many delays meant they were going up in monsoon
conditions; the other team members had frostbite, and at
the summit Herzog spent too much time and they ended
up having to bivouac in a crevasse during a storm. 'It
is not just about reaching a goal. You should be strong
enough and wise enough to say no at some point to save
the situation. You have to know your limit, know that
going beyond that fine line will put you and your team in
jeopardy,' he says.

Gaurav and Siddharth had just turned thirty and were
thriving in the corporate world in which they had spent
close to eight years each. But the pull of being their own
bosses and building and enlarging a brand of their own was
too strong to resist. Early in 2007, Siddharth had come to
India to visit Gaurav's newborn daughter and they discussed
Dinesh's suggestion.

'Sid and I both had the itch to leave our corporate
careers. I felt I was getting quite complacent. I had been
talking to Dinesh regularly about Wildcraft and had a
good sense of it. I was at the stage where I felt I really had
to give Wildcraft a shot, because it had so much promise,
or let it go for good,' says Gaurav. 'It was a now-or-never
moment.'

Siddharth weighed his options and decided to throw in his lot with Dinesh and Gaurav rather than follow the assured career path ahead of him. He went back to Kuala Lumpur, resigned from Hewitt Associates and joined Wildcraft, full-time, in July 2007. Gaurav made the switch from Standard Chartered in December 2007.

'My first day at Wildcraft was probably the most unproductive day in my entire career so far,' says Siddharth, who is brisk and forthcoming and talks at the rate of about five words a second. 'I didn't know head or tail about anything or anybody. There was no induction programme or any of those things you have in large companies. There is no agenda—you are responsible for the strategic agenda, the tactical agenda as well as your daily agenda. I was at sea during my first month there. What I handled as daily revenue at my previous company was the entire annual revenue here.' He started immersing himself in every aspect of the business, spending a lot of time at the Jayanagar store to understand the customers and the market demand.

'I enjoyed turning my brain to new challenges. There is this very romanticized view of working for yourself and creating value, but the reality is hard work. Suddenly, all the things you are used to—swanky office, salary, office staff, even air-conditioning—go away,' says Siddharth. The Wildcraft office is still without air-conditioning, in part because Bangalore's weather doesn't demand it, but mainly because the corporate office and factory floor share the same space. 'It is not easy to make the transition though I consider it the best decision I have made in my life. You have to really be committed to growing a business, and have internal drive. You cannot have a plan B; there is only plan A,' says Siddharth.

Once Gaurav joined, they spent the first twenty-four months testing the market. Until then, Wildcraft had been largely a Bangalore brand and it was left to be seen whether it was possible to take the brand pan-national. Stores were opened in Pune and Hyderabad to test the waters. No revenue targets were set for the first two years, but Siddharth and Gaurav started putting systems and processes in place for everything, from recruitment and procurement to stocking and pricing.

'We drew a broad picture of what we wanted, but we were first-time entrepreneurs and had a lot to learn. All the planning we had done before was in a structured corporate environment in which you do not consider capital as a constraint. When you're an entrepreneur, capital is the main challenge, so you can't set out cash flows and business plans the way large corporates do,' says Gaurav.

Further, they had no direct competitor and did not know the size of their market. They began gathering data on the adventure, travel and sports sectors and started keeping track of who bought their products and for what uses. Finally, in 2009, they drew up a detailed business plan with the aim of being a Rs 50-crore brand by 2011.

When Gaurav and Siddharth joined in 2007–08, Wildcraft was a twenty-five-person manufacturing facility. Since then, they've grown to more than 2000 employees, a majority of them still production staff. In 2011, Wildcraft opened another manufacturing facility in Solan in Himachal Pradesh to reach markets in the north faster. In September 2013, Silicon Valley-based venture capital fund Sequoia Capital invested in the company. Wildcraft touched Rs 100 crore in 2012–13 and is now setting its sights on being a Rs 500-crore brand by 2017–18.

Dinesh, Gaurav and Siddharth have their offices on the second floor of a nondescript five-storey building in Uttarahalli, where Wildcraft's second coming took off in 2003. The office-cum-factory is spread over 60,000 sq. ft across two buildings and two warehouses. Dinesh assists in product design, Gaurav helps in marketing and sales, and Siddharth is the finance and operations guy. In a huge space divided by glass walls, flat-screen monitors sit on white tables, wilted potted palms laze by the windows and, incongruously, a couple of dusty fake rocks are scattered around. On the third floor is a large airy workshop with about a dozen sewing machines, half-sewn backpacks lying on cutting tables, spools of coloured thread in trays against the window and finished backpacks hanging from hooks waiting to head out to the mountains. There's something genteel and old-worldly about that sewing room that contrasts with the glassiness of the office one floor below and the rugged yet slick image seen in stores and advertisements, and it seems to point to the marriage of aggressive top-line growth and a deep love for the outdoors that Wildcraft symbolizes.

Today, Wildcraft is a company that's a curious combination of the two kinds of people that drive enterprise. One is the person who sees an opportunity and grabs it, whose driving mission is to create a company by providing a product or service that fulfils a particular need or demand, and watches it grow. Gaurav and Siddharth are the people who saw an opportunity for growth in Wildcraft and made the risky jump into the business. The other kind of entrepreneur is like Dinesh—someone driven by a love for something and has faith in a seemingly impractical dream. Both kinds of people are self-motivated, conscientious and determined, yet the driving force is different and the kind of passion—though not really comparable—each brings to the enterprise is different. Wildcraft is an unusual case of both kinds of entrepreneurs, though of different ages and ideas, comfortably sharing the same table. All three hold the designation of director and consult one another on all decisions, though each is aware of his own expertise and limitations.

'The perspective to grow this company came from its core value—integrity of people and product, which Dinesh had put in place,' says Siddharth. 'We maintained that, built systems around it and brought much-needed order to the way it was run.'

Dinesh agrees that the ethos of the company has not changed though everything else around it has. 'The whole outdoor culture that bred Wildcraft has changed. In the initial years, we made and tested the products ourselves. In the West, companies like Patagonia and The North Face are staffed by people who are passionate about the outdoors. I had to come to terms with the fact that that customer base here is very small and that few Indians are adventurers in that sense,' he says. He takes his staff on trekking and climbing trips once a quarter to try and inculcate the same love for the outdoors he has, on the foundation of which the company was founded when he was in his thirties.

'Drifting through your twenties and thirties without a proper job was not at all acceptable in the 1980s,' says Dinesh, who is fifty-four now. 'It's not totally acceptable even now, but at least people will understand if you tell them you want to do something that you love. And climbing mountains? People thought I was crazy!'

During the first ten years of Wildcraft and his time in the US, Dinesh's parents kept a worried eye on him. 'They did not show their displeasure openly, but you could see they were wondering what the hell I was doing. I never agreed to get married because I wanted to figure out what I wanted to do with my life,' he says.

Even after the company took off, Dinesh's parents felt that a lot of time had been wasted. 'That's always there; that's the thing with individuals and society and how you measure success. If you're doing something that gives you satisfaction and happiness, is that tangible? Is that success? Can we measure it? I don't know. If you measure a person's success by the amount of money stashed away in the bank, then you can say I have been a failure for so long. For me, success has meant going after what I wanted and never giving up. Bringing adventure activities to India, going to all the wild places, all the learning, starting this enterprise and seeing people be appreciative, that has given me satisfaction. Now the company has started doing well and I see the benefits and the money. The flip side is, yes, I have given up a lot, but I have no regrets . . . absolutely no regrets.'

Dinesh no longer holds the majority stake and has handed over the reins of the day-to-day operations to Gaurav and Siddharth, though he still has the last word on product design. 'In the last seven years, the company has grown more than a hundred times. One hundred times! That's something!' says Dinesh. 'Of course, I laid the foundation, but they've scaled it up further than I ever could have. They're extremely hard-working and passionate, and I know the company is in safe hands,' he says. And then the wicked side of him comes out: 'They're very serious,' he says, his deep laugh filling the room. 'And I want to be free to go on trips whenever I want to. After all, adventure is my business.'

DINESH'S TIPS TO SCALE THE SUMMIT

1. You have to be passionate; use your head to follow your heart, work hard and persevere; there are no shortcuts.
2. Always be in touch with what drives you; make sure you know what you are working for.
3. Have a clear goal and work towards it, but you should also be strong enough and wise enough to say no at some point to save the situation. You have to know your limit, know that going beyond that fine line will put you and your team in jeopardy.

A PENCHANT FOR SUITS

Mahesh and Suresh Ramakrishnan

Mahesh and Suresh Ramakrishnan train underprivileged men and women in Tamil Nadu and Andhra Pradesh to craft bespoke suits that retail on Savile Row in London. The twins fell in love with fine clothing while they worked in the corporate world in New York, and have now built their own world-class brand.

Suresh Ramakrishnan leads the way down a narrow, angular staircase in a 100-year-old house on St George Street in London that has housed fine-tailoring firms since 1911. He tells a story of the landlord's father being the legendary Savile Row tailor who was the inspiration for John le Carré's *The Tailor of Panama*. The building is centrally heated, keeping out the autumn chill and the little noise of London's streets. Suresh straightens the tie of his perfectly cut slate-grey suit and opens the door to the tailoring room. He points out the eighty-year-old deep-blue carpet covering the floor that you want to tiptoe across for fear of disturbing the tailors, quietly stitching grey tweed and merino wool with precision. They're sitting on stools at wide, white-topped worktables, snipping, measuring, stitching and sketching, making suits for some of the world's best-dressed men.

Half a world away, his twin, Mahesh Ramakrishnan, dressed in brown linen trousers and a pale-blue shirt, points through the banisters of the wide staircase in a bungalow in Chennai's Mahalingapuram to the tailoring room below. A warm breeze blows in from the street and crows create a cacophony in the background. Cars honk on Kodambakkam bridge a few kilometres away and there's the occasional rumble of a passing suburban train. The tailors look up, smile, chat and show the perfectly spaced stitches and neat cuts they're making in grey tweed and merino wool. They're sitting on stools at wide, white-topped worktables, snipping, measuring, stitching and sketching, making suits for some of the world's best-dressed men.

The Ramakrishnan brothers run Whitcomb & Shaftesbury, a bespoke tailoring company that works between Chennai and London, producing fine, handmade suits in the tradition of Savile Row, which is known for the world's best tailoring. The British tailors in London craft 'Savile Row Bespoke' suits that retail upwards of £3000 (around Rs 3 lakh), while the unit in Chennai creates the less expensive 'Classic Bespoke' line that starts at £1360 (approximately Rs 1.3 lakh). Both are sold from the hushed rooms on the top floor of the house on St George Street in London. The brothers also run a unit in Tada on the Andhra Pradesh border to train underprivileged women in bespoke tailoring—the craft of customizing clothing to an individual based on hundreds of precise measurements.

Whitcomb & Shaftesbury's clientele includes heads of state and corporate leaders, rock stars and sports stars, British peers and Italian counts, and celebrities and luminaries of all shades—names that would make you draw a breath or raise an eyebrow. While Mahesh, the oldest of the triplets—the third brother, Ganesh, is an anthropologist—takes care of the Chennai and Tada units, Suresh is in London, meeting clients, travelling to widen the customer base and keeping an eagle eye on the accounts.

About fifteen years ago, Mahesh and Suresh didn't imagine they'd be tailors. The brothers, now in their early forties, were living in New York—Mahesh, a managing director responsible for strategy projects with IT consulting firm Sapient, and Suresh a vice president at Goldman Sachs after a stint as a venture capitalist in Silicon Valley. They wore suits to work every day, shopped for the finest quality coats and trousers, and loved the idea of being perfectly turned out. 'In the mid-1990s, when we landed our first jobs, the workplace was very formal,' says Mahesh. 'And what we both loved about it was that when you got dressed up in a suit, your mind was completely focused on work. When you came home and changed, you relaxed. I found my mind was switching on and off based purely on how I was dressed, and I loved that,' he says.

Until then, at the University of Rochester in New York, the brothers had been mucking around in T-shirts and jeans, studying economics and information sciences after finishing school in Chennai. Being so far from home meant they learned to make their own decisions and do things their own way. When everyone else in class was doing set degrees, the brothers found their niche in the upcoming area of computer information systems and decided to switch majors from engineering.

'Back then, the university didn't offer a degree in information systems—it was so new. So Suresh and I worked with the faculty in the computer science department to create our own degrees. It's a lot of work, but we wanted it,' says Mahesh, sipping black tea, sitting in a cane chair on a balcony that extends out of his office room in Chennai.

They graduated in 1995 and Mahesh joined the technology company Sapient, while Suresh took up finance and joined Goldman Sachs. 'Everyone says America is the land of opportunity, but we used to add, "You really have to slog for it,"' says Suresh over a pint at the Windmill in London, the pub at the end of Savile Row, where all the tailors and cutters gather for a drink and a gossip after work. At the next table, four tailors in coats Bertie Wooster would envy are discussing a football match. Suresh, cricket-mad like his brother, surfaces after checking a test match score on his iPhone and continues, 'Sorry, India's not doing so well, but where was I? Yes, the work was hard and the hours long, but the environment was fantastic.'

While Suresh climbed the ladder in financial management and eventually went to Wharton for an MBA, Mahesh's star was on the rise in the IT field, because Sapient, which he joined as a start-up, had gone public, making employee stock options worth millions of dollars. He moved to other companies and eventually re-joined Sapient in 2003 to start its India office in Gurgaon.

'At that point, my wife and I were keen to return to India,' says Mahesh. 'I had spent most of my growing-up and work years in the US. I wanted to move back, but was nervous because the work environment would be different, so this seemed like a good opportunity to test the waters.'

Throughout all the years of switching jobs, consulting clients, building careers and making money, the fascination for good suits was a constant. When they left for college, the brothers had got their suits tailored at Raymond in Chennai, like all other students, choosing the best fabric that the sales staff recommended. 'After our first year at work, when we got our bonuses, we went to buy some new clothes,' says Suresh. The range bewildered them: the prices soared from $300 to $8000, but the suits all looked and felt the same. They chanced upon two Armani suits that seemed identical in all aspects except for the price tags—one read $700, the other $3000. That's when the light bulb went on: Is there more to a suit than just the fabric?

It was a question that led them into a whole new world. 'We read, chatted with the sales staff, met tailors, pumped everybody we could for information,' says Mahesh. They started learning about the kinds of fabric, the difference between a fused suit (where the canvas and fabric are just ironed together, which is what most ready-made suits are) and a canvas suit (a delicate assembly of fabric, canvas, wadding and horsehair stitched with silk thread to take the shape of the body, which Savile Row specializes in), and what 'the perfect fit' really means.

As their paycheques became bigger, they moved on to luxury brands, to tailored suits, and eventually reached Savile Row, the Mecca for the Well-Dressed Man. 'If you think about synonyms across sectors, it's Japanese electronics, Swiss watches, German automobiles—and English suits. Savile Row is the epitome of the craft of bespoke tailoring,' says Mahesh.

On Savile Row, suit-making is an art perfected over 300 years. The earliest tailors made uniforms for the military, where the purpose was to create outfits that would make the army look indomitable. So the shoulders were squared, the chests broadened, and the overall look was one of might and authority. The tailors, with their fine understanding of body structure, became experts at camouflaging flaws to create a look of uniform strength. Over time, the military greatcoats were shortened and refashioned into the modern suit with a short jacket and trousers. And it was the English who perfected this art of fitting and kitting out men.

Since then the Italians have learnt the art of tailoring and have cut the trade into two spheres: they are the masters of mass-produced, ready-made suits using lightweight material, and the English have remained the smaller artisanal makers of custom clothing. It's this tradition of perfection that the brothers are now teaching to underprivileged men and women in India.

'A good suit should camouflage your flaws and play up your strengths because nobody is perfect except for half a dozen genetic freaks,' says Mahesh. 'It's an art and also a craft.' Apart from a detailed knowledge of the human anatomy, there's the need to understand how different fabrics behave under varying climatic conditions, and the intricacies of suit construction. 'The human body is made up of so many parts that you have to study anatomy for six to eight months. Then there are the different stitches, how to cut, how to construct the different layers so that the suit becomes a three-dimensional object that moves with your body. It was a curiosity that became a hobby that became a passion,' says Mahesh.

Their love for fine clothing led them to forge friendships with some of the best cutters and tailors on the Row, including John McCabe and Thomas Mahon, who were happy to give them more information. 'We considered getting into it, but I wondered whether we could break into such a closed business. We're the Ramakrishnan brothers. This is a centuries-old British tradition,' says Mahesh.

In his final year at Wharton in 2003, one of Suresh's projects involved developing a business idea. 'My proposal was to set up a fine tailoring business with a social aspect. Mahesh helped develop the idea and, at the end of it, we thought: Why not try it for real?' Suresh says.

One of the things they decided on from the very beginning—and the unique feature of the project that caught the attention of Suresh's professors at Wharton—was that they would build a company that integrated the best elements of the systems, processes and values that they had experienced in their corporate life. 'From manufacture and order systems that eliminated surplus to the creation of a unique labour force which would one day be recognized across the world—these were ideas we worked hard to combine,' says Suresh.

Both were motivated by the desire to do something that they could look back on and be proud of in twenty-five years. 'We wanted to create something that the world would notice, while making a real difference in people's lives. Yes, we were making an impact in our own lives, but how were we really helping others not as fortunate?' says Suresh. 'That was one of the major drivers behind us deciding to build a company based on human beings rather than machine labour.' Both wanted the business to have a social angle, inspired by their mother, Usha Ramakrishnan, who has worked with the disabled for most of her life. But the fear of leaving a successful career dogged Mahesh till the brothers and their wives decided to take a holiday together in Paris.

'All we could talk about was setting up the business,' says Suresh. 'I didn't want to go back to banking. I had an offer from Goldman Sachs again, but I couldn't imagine sitting behind a desk doing a routine job. I knew we had to try it then or we'd never do it.' He had enjoyed working, but realized that his banking jobs were pushing him to pursue goals and live a lifestyle he didn't want. 'More money makes you want to live as per others' ideals. People who realize this early on are better equipped to find other parts of their lives that are more fulfiling,' he says.

Mahesh concedes that a résumé with more than ten years of work experience and a tidy sum in the bank made him believe that he could afford the risk. 'There is no perfect time to make the very hard decisions. You just have to make them. You can't build a business while working in another,' he says.

Suresh, who like his brother has two children, adds, 'Neither of us had children at that point, so I think taking a decision to quit and become tailors was easier.' It also helped that the brothers had each other to bounce off ideas, fears and doubts, bolster spirits and keep away the blues. 'The more we talked about it, the more possible it seemed. Why couldn't we do this in India?'

In the global market, India is seen as a place with excellent skills and knowledge but questionable commitment to quality. 'Through our work life, we found that India is considered a back-end place, whether in IT or the garments business, not a destination for great quality. There is no reason why Indian goods cannot be as good as the best in the world. We wanted to do something to change this perception of India,' Mahesh says. The story of Japanese electronics giant Sony, which single-handedly changed the perception of Japan as a maker of cheap electronics, was their inspiration. 'It was a naive thought, but one that drove us,' he says.

With suit-making, the business would always be small and niche. 'But it was a good way to prove that skills and quality can go hand in hand in India. The people who get tailored at Savile Row are the cream of society—social, political and economic leaders. Who better to prove it to?' says Mahesh.

By the beginning of 2004, Mahesh had quit and the brothers began laying the groundwork for their business. They worked on a business plan, set up partnerships with friends on Savile Row, and convinced their parents and in-laws that they knew what they were doing. 'Our wives were for it, they knew our hearts were in it—after all, they had suffered us going in and out of shops for years,' says Suresh, laughing. 'But my in-laws were rather hesitant. Being entrepreneurs themselves, they knew the difficulties, and it's only now that I understand and appreciate their concerns and fears,' he says.

In December 2004, a devastating tsunami pounded the eastern coast of India, washing away lives, families, homes and livelihoods, and leaving survivors scarred. The brothers' friend Jean-Francois Lesage, of a French embroidery house, who works with craftsmen in Chennai, suggested that they help with a tailoring rehabilitation programme for tsunami survivors, which his charity Children of the World wanted to run.

'We had incorporated our company, but we didn't have a running business. We were considering buying an existing business in the UK, building it up with our contacts in the US, and setting up the India arm later,' says Mahesh. But Lesage's request had them drawing a new pattern.

It was an opportunity to help others and set up the India unit they had discussed. 'It was just happening differently from what we'd planned,' says Suresh. They set up a workshop in Chennai and a three-year rehabilitation programme with the help of local tailors, and cutters and suit-makers from London who had become friends and wanted to do their bit for the tsunami survivors.

The specialists from London would come down for three weeks to a month and train the local tailors and the survivors. 'It was great training for us too because we were seeing the craft up close and learning the little details,' says Mahesh, demonstrating the right way to hold a needle, loop the thread around the little finger and draw it through while making a stitch so that the tension is just right.

Over the next three years, 120 tsunami survivors passed through the workshop, picking up the craft of creating a suit. All the garments made during those early years were given away because they didn't make the cut. 'Making an international-quality garment is about following certain techniques. It's the last 10 per cent of the work that makes all the difference. That is 90 per cent of the effort. We were very clear about quality and were not willing to compromise,' says Mahesh. The trainees were given cloth, canvas, horsehair and wadding to cut, assemble and stitch, rare in the business because it's quite expensive, coming to more than Rs 2000 a suit. The brothers absorbed most of the costs of the training programme.

'It didn't make financial sense, of course,' says Mahesh. 'You don't start a business by giving away things, but it was something we knew we had to do for people who had lost so much, and how would they learn if they didn't work on the real thing?' Many had never seen a suit before, so both men and women were encouraged to try on coats to understand how it felt to wear one so that they could fashion them better.

Many of the young women left to get married, the men returned to the sea once they recovered, some got poached by established suit-makers, a few struck out on their own and set up small tailoring businesses. About ten stayed on and have become valued craftspeople, sewing suits that retail on Savile Row. 'We wanted to provide people an opportunity and a skill, which we think we did. Whether they stayed or left was their choice,' says Mahesh. 'Suresh and I worked with the idea that not a single trainee would stay on. It was a gamble, but one for a good reason.'

Simultaneously, they worked on the British end of Whitcomb & Shaftesbury, setting up an entirely new firm, which opened for business by the end of 2006. That was another challenge because one can't just recruit tailors on Savile Row; they're more like sophisticated guns for hire, picking specific jobs that suit them. Each one is a specialist—cutter, coat-maker, waistcoat-maker, trouser-maker—and each has a seamless relationship with the other. They work in groups and the firm has its own relationship with these groups. The customer base too is built through relationships and recommendations, not advertising or marketing. 'This business is a bit like private banking—whether staff or customers, people only come on recommendations. There are no walk-ins,' says Suresh.

The British name is one that often raises questions, considering the brothers are making a push for Indian quality. 'Most of the firms on Savile Row are a hundred years old. We had no history, no base. We knew Indian tailoring is good, but a store with the name "Ramakrishnan Bros" isn't going to inspire confidence in the English upper class. We had enough to swim against without having to explain how to pronounce a non-English name as well,' says Mahesh. So the business became Whitcomb & Shaftesbury, impishly named after two streets in central London's Soho, a once-grungy nightlife district that's turned fashionably upmarket.

Their first clients were friends and acquaintances from their working life in New York. Suresh had done a stint in London with Goldman Sachs in his previous avatar and tapped into contacts there too. The credibility they had built as professionals for a decade, and the reputation they had gained for knowing their suits by giving colleagues tips on workwear, stood them in good stead. 'They knew we were mad about suits and were happy to invest in our clothes, but we did worry about whom we would sell to once we exhausted the circle of friends,' says Suresh.

Fortunately, their friends told friends and business began picking up slowly. The working end seemed to divide itself naturally—Mahesh, with his background in strategic planning and operations and base in India, took care of the Chennai workshop, while Suresh, the financial planner, looked after the London end of meeting clients and tailors and keeping the firm in the black.

By the end of 2008, the tsunami rehabilitation programme was winding down and the brothers were wondering if the workshop in Chennai would ever sustain itself. While the tailors had picked up skills, their work didn't match Savile Row standards and the suits were still being given to friends and family.

That's when another friend, Ravi Reddy, came to them with a request. He'd set up a special economic zone in Tada, on the border of Tamil Nadu and Andhra Pradesh, and under the government rules, had to provide employment for the locals. But most companies in the SEZ only had housekeeping and security jobs for the unskilled men and women. Would the brothers consider running a similar training programme there?

Mahesh and Suresh met some locals and social workers and realized that gender inequality and domestic abuse were high. 'So we decided on a programme for women. Again, it was a social decision, not a business one,' says Suresh. So the Chennai workshop was turned into a specialized tailoring unit with the few trained tailors who had weathered the tsunami, and the training programme moved to the SEZ.

The idea was to create a line of suits in the Chennai workshop that would meet the exacting Savile Row standards. The Classic Bespoke line follows the same fitting process as the Savile Row Bespoke. Customers are measured and fitted in London, and the cutter creates the pattern there. The pattern, cloth and trimmings are sent to Chennai for assembly. The assembled suit is sent back and forth, between London and Chennai, for the customer to try, and changes are made for a perfect fit. It may seem a bit complicated, but the result is a Savile Row suit at half the price.

The moment they told clients in London that they were planning to sell 'Made in India' suits on Savile Row, they caused a bit of a scandal. 'No one would believe the quality could match up. They thought it was impossible,' says Suresh. Many regular customers who swore by their British-made suits told the brothers that they would never wear suits made in a small city in south India. But the brothers believed they could make a go of it.

A couple of months after the individual meetings with Mahesh and Suresh, we're all on the road to Tada, about 70 km from Chennai, where the brothers have been running the training programme since 2009. In Chennai, it's all men on the floor; in London, there's a mix of men and women, though men are in the majority; but at Tada, thirty women fill the white worktables, stitching flaps and buttonholes and carefully steaming canvas and cloth. There are just four men on the floor—the master trouser-maker, two senior coat-makers, and the centre head, responsible for quality control.

'It takes about three years to train a tailor to international standards,' says Suresh. 'You don't get any value during that time, and after the three years of training, they might just leave.' The women go through a three-phase programme after which they can make a coat and trousers. Each phase stretches for nine months, during which they get a stipend. The first phase is largely about grooming, discipline and the basics of stitching. 'Many drop out halfway through the first phase because they've never held a regular job and cannot get used to the discipline of daily work and systems,' says Mahesh.

In the second phase, women learn to make components like collars, zips, flaps and buttonholes. In the third, they begin assembling a coat or trousers. Once they finish, they can choose to join the unit full-time or strike out on their own. 'At Goldman Sachs, we had a 360-degree review system. Your peers would review you as would your bosses, and juniors would review the bosses. It's a system we follow at Tada,' says Suresh.

Pride in work isn't just something Mahesh and Suresh have; every person at the Tada workshop is inordinately proud of what they do. The women eagerly display the trousers or collar or buttonhole they're working on, and are quick to demonstrate and explain the finesse of the technique they're using. 'There's so much to learn because it's not just about following the steps. It's also about the nuances of each step,' says twenty-eight-year-old Subharani, who lives in a village nearby with her two children. 'For instance, a sleeve has to have looser stitches in front and tighter ones behind for easy movement,' she says. Initially, Subharani's family refused to believe she was stitching garments that were sold abroad, but were happy to let her work as the stipend was welcome. 'Only when John sir [head-cutter John McCabe] came from London to train us and visited our village did they believe me,' she says.

Mindset is something Mahesh works on every day. 'Their [trainees'] egos are fragile because they've always been told that they're good for nothing. I have to keep reassuring them that they can compete with the best in the world and that they should be proud of every single thing they do,' he says. 'To strive for excellence, people have to be proud of what they do.'

Tailors from London come in every three months to reinforce lessons and ensure that things don't loosen up. About 400 women have gone through the programme at Tada. Many have got married, stopped working because of family problems or started their own businesses, but thirty have stayed. 'We're hoping to have about sixty women working full-time for us here, but we'll have to be patient,' says Mahesh.

Patience has been the defining factor of this business. In 2011, a full five years after it started, the Chennai workshop sent its first suits out to Savile Row under the Classic Bespoke label. The British tailors are also changing their minds about Indian quality. 'A little over a year ago, when the Indian suits started coming out, if customers asked me what the difference between the two lines was, I would say Classic Bespoke is 70 per cent of the quality at 50 per cent of the cost,' says John McCabe, Whitcomb & Shaftesbury's head cutter. 'Two weeks ago, a customer from Luxembourg came in and asked that same question. I said 90 per cent of the quality at 50 per cent of the cost,' says McCabe.

It is a rather audacious idea to get men and women from villages who have never worn anything but saris and *veshti*s to tailor suits for boardroom moguls. 'We didn't get into this business to make cut-price suits. We got into it because we loved the craft and we wanted to have people understand the sense of achievement that comes from creating the best quality,' says Suresh.

The Tada workshop has started working on 'white labelled suits', trade parlance for bulk orders for ready-made suits undertaken for another brand. Though the Tada unit is primarily a social enterprise, it is registered as a for-profit enterprise, MSR Garments, and costs them £2000 (about Rs 2 lakh) a month to run. 'We're putting in the money, but not making profits on it yet,' says Suresh. The Chennai unit has just started breaking even, while the UK business is in the black. The brothers also travel to the US often to meet clients and get orders.

'The hardest part of this has been the uncertainty. Just because today is a good day, tomorrow might not be,' says Suresh. The first three years were the worst when none of the units were making money and the brothers were drawing entirely on their savings.

Mahesh says he still misses the surety of a monthly paycheque. 'No matter what, I would get money when I was working,' he says. 'Now, you have one fantastic month, but for the next two months, there's no money at all. You can't stop spending, though, because you still have to pay salaries to the people who work for you. That uncertainty is something that takes getting used to, and I'm more comfortable with it now.'

The camaraderie of the workplace is another thing Mahesh misses. 'To some extent, I miss interaction with peers. Suresh deals with customers in the shop so he doesn't feel it. I get my dose of it when I travel, but on a day-to-day basis, I'm here and once I give instructions, I don't have anyone to interact with. I do the rounds and check on the work, but I'm always the boss,' he says, laughing. 'Sounds fantastic, but it isn't. You don't have anyone to bounce an idea off or just talk. Sometimes I wonder if I am missing something because there is no one else to see what I'm doing.'

If you measure success entirely in monetary terms, the brothers aren't doing badly, plus they are far happier than they were in regular jobs. 'We make decisions that make us happy, and that, for us, is success. We have more time for our families, we choose how we work and what our work leads to,' says Suresh.

Mahesh adds, 'It's been a hard time, sacrifices have been made, but it's starting to come together. We have felt the pressure, the financial and the social pressure, but I've never felt like I'm coming in to work, because we're truly passionate about quality and the craft. We asked ourselves: If we had all the money in the world, what would we do? —and the answer is this.'

A decade on, they still face the occasional question about Indian quality. Recently, a British peer, who's been buying their Savile Row Bespoke suits, felt the material and examined the detailing on a suit on a mannequin at the London store and told Suresh, 'Your suits made in India may be nice, but I'm sure they'll never be as good as this one.' 'I said, "That is made in India",' Suresh relates. The customer bought the suit. 'Seeing is believing. When they see the quality, they change their minds.'

Early in 2014, the brothers entered the Indian market by retailing bespoke suits through luxury design and fashion chain Evoluzione in Chennai. They're also replicating the Savile Row experience in Chennai in partnership with Evoluzione with a store modelled on their London showroom, complete with the hushed look and feel of a gentlemen's lounge.

In July that year, they unveiled a co-branded line of ethnic wear with designer Tarun Tahiliani. While Tahiliani designed the collection of thirteen *sherwani*s and *bandhgala*s, which are available in his couture studios, Whitcomb & Shaftesbury provides the fabrics from London and is doing all the tailoring at its Chennai workshop.

In a sense, this collaboration, which was worked out over two years, between an Indian fashion designer and a Savile Row tailoring firm, is a return to roots since structured garments like the sherwani and bandhgala were introduced during the British Raj as court dress. Since then, sherwanis have become heavy, ungainly outfits with a profusion of sparkly and elaborate embroidery to conceal flaws in fitting and cutting. 'The inspiration is to create more contemporary and comfortable Indian men's wear by bringing together the best of Indian design with Savile Row-quality tailoring and cutting,' says Mahesh.

The brothers say there's far more to do and learn. 'The scale of what we are trying to do is a bit limiting. In our line, one project is one suit,' says Suresh. Apart from building up the Chennai workshop and keeping the rich, famous and influential coming to the Savile Row shop, they want the Tada unit to have full-time staff and start a second training programme.

And there's the desire for more fun at work. 'We'd like to meet Rahul Dravid. We admire his mental attitude and his relentless pursuit of perfection, which is a paradigm we follow,' says Mahesh. 'We'd be really excited if he called us!'

TAILOR-MADE ADVICE

1. Have values, vision, a clear goal and a purpose for your company, and stick to it. Ours is clear: We want to make the best suits in the world at a reasonable cost in an ethical, socially responsible way; and we want to change people's perception of quality in India. Everything we've achieved is because we've stuck to the vision and sacrificed anything that might interfere with it, including profits, the option of doing things faster and cheaper, or closing the rehab programme.

2. Be aware of the challenges. Even if you do everything properly, things may not work out.

3. The life of an entrepreneur can be lonely. We are lucky to have each other. To do it alone is very hard, so be prepared for that.

FINDING HER WAY ON THE ROAD

Piya Bose

Piya Bose quit her job as a corporate lawyer because she loved to travel and took off on a road trip to Tibet. She returned to Mumbai, wanting to share the experience with other women, and set up Girls on the Go, a company that plans trips across the world exclusively for women.

The clock struck 3 a.m. as she sat in a tiny filing room, sleepily locating and scanning documents to meet the deadline for the legal due diligence on a transaction for the law firm she worked at. For more than a week, she had been cooped up in the small room and, in the dim light, the wall-to-wall filing cabinets seemed to close in on her. Over and over, her exhausted brain asked her why she chose to remain dwarfed by a mountain of legal documents on a seemingly endless graveyard shift, when she could be scaling a real mountain somewhere else. With no thought but of escape, she hauled herself out of the room, walked up to the desk of her unappreciative senior associate and resigned.

The next morning Piya Bose woke up to realize what she had done. She was twenty-five and it was just over a year since she had moved to Mumbai to begin her career as a corporate lawyer in one of the country's top law firms. She had less than a month's salary left in her bank account and had no idea what to do next.

'It was a bit impulsive, but I had plunged into the dark because I could not continue in a job that required no originality. I needed to find my light at the end of the tunnel. Going back was not an option,' says Piya.

Like most office drones, Piya had spent hours at her computer dreaming of being on a cruise in the Mediterranean or relaxing in a deckchair on a gorgeous beach, trying to forget the fact that she had to draft contracts for a living. She had been travelling alone from the time she was sixteen, when she was selected for a student exchange programme to Brazil. 'Until then, I had never even gone to tuition classes alone. That trip taught me to stand on my own feet. I realized that there is so much to learn and see in this world. All I wanted to do was travel,' she says.

Instead of pursuing her love for English literature after she finished school in Jamshedpur—India's steel city, where every other person is a doctor or an engineer—she followed the crowd like most confused eighteen-year-olds and chose a professional course that would guarantee a well-paying job at the end of five years and make her parents happy. 'I was motivated by everything except what I was about to study—the biggest mistake most students make,' she says.

Piya's love for literature persisted. Her favourite course in law school was 'Law and Literature', and for one of her projects, she chose the subject 'Legal Literature in *Asterix*

Comics'. The only accolade that came her way in law school was a first prize for poetry, though the other subjects that interested her were space law, intellectual property rights and maritime law. Soon after getting her LLB (BSc) degree from the National University of Juridical Sciences (NUJS), Kolkata, in 2006, she was recruited by one of India's top law firms for its Mumbai office. But, as she accepted her hefty signing bonus, instead of feeling elated, she felt a deep void.

'My parents were so happy. I was earning more than Rs 80,000 a month at my first job,' says Piya, who was born in 1982 and raised in Jamshedpur. The money went quickly— on food, short trips and shopping—to counter the gloom of realizing that her heart was not in her work. As a student she had done exciting internships with the Ministry of Information Technology in New Delhi and with a panellist from the World Intellectual Property Organization (WIPO) in Kuala Lumpur. 'But my full-time job required very little application of mind, so those five years of studying the law seemed useless. I was bored and frustrated.'

Piya found it more absorbing to plan trips for herself and her friends. On a dare, she figured out a land route from Mumbai to London and set out the entire itinerary for a disbelieving colleague. 'My greatest understanding of myself came as I sat at my work desk for hours dreaming about seeing the world. I didn't want to be tied down to a desk and a place,' she says.

To ease the monotony, she began writing travelogues for newspapers and magazines about her adventures in South America, the US, the UK and India. The money wasn't much—just about Rs 3000 an article—compared to the hourly rates associates like her charged in the law firm, but it made her happy. 'It was a real high to see my name in print. For the first time I realized I could earn money doing something I enjoyed. It opened up the possibility of a career in travel-writing, even if it meant a drastic cut in my paycheque,' she says.

She signed up on Couchsurfing.com, a hospitality site for travellers that works on a non-monetary, pay-it-forward principle and encourages members to stay with one another while they are on the road. Piya often ended up providing bed and board for young, single women from other countries and always felt a twinge of jealousy that they were travelling the world with just a backpack. 'Why couldn't I do that? Why weren't any Indian women doing that, I would ask myself,' she says.

Sharing her home with women from around the world opened up her mind not only to new cultures but also to ideas and experiences. She slowly began to understand that the way in which a society views travel is also important. 'Abroad, students are encouraged to travel during their holidays, volunteer in foreign countries or take a gap year to see the world,' she says. 'It's a habit that starts early and it shapes your world view. It's not considered strange or irresponsible for them, as it is here, to quit a job just to travel for a year.'

After a point, armchair travel and vicarious living just wasn't enough. The question that began eating away at her was: Do I stick with this life of earning close to Rs 1 lakh a month as a twenty-five-year-old? Or do I give it all up and try to do what I really want?

She knew she was tired of the firm, but thought she would give herself some time to figure out what to do next. 'I was 100 per cent sure that life as it was at that point was not making me happy, but I couldn't make up my mind about quitting. The physical and mental claustrophobia of that filing room finally pushed me over the edge. That was my tipping point.'

The day after she quit in March 2007 was also when she realized that she would have to make quite a few changes in her lifestyle. 'I would take a cab from my house in Worli to my office every day and think nothing of the expense because the firm covered it. Instead, I started enjoying the wait at the bus stop, using that time to sit, think and watch the world go by,' she says.

She spent that first month just being a tourist in Mumbai, a city she had moved to a year ago, but had had very little time to explore and make her own by discovering its hidden treasures. 'I walked a lot more. I loved the city and had more time to enjoy it. You can live life king-size at any rung of the ladder.'

About a month later, she went to Lucknow, planning to travel to Himachal Pradesh with her friend and fellow travel enthusiast Aadil Desai, who would later become her husband and greatest supporter. In Lucknow, she met a cycle-rickshaw driver who suggested she go to Nepal rather than Himachal Pradesh since they were so close to the Sunauli border. The two friends found they could afford this and they also had their passports, so they set off overland for Nepal.

In Kathmandu, travel agents were advertising trips to Tibet. Piya did some quick calculations and realized that she would be spending all her savings on one trip, but decided to book herself on a tour anyway. 'It was the best decision of my life,' she says.

It was her first long trip after the one she had taken to Brazil when she was sixteen. She crossed mountain passes, traced the course of the Brahmaputra River and eventually stood right in front of Mount Everest at Tingri. That month-long trip turned out to be Piya's proverbial life-changing experience, giving her a real understanding of how travel shaped her view of the world. 'You can't see the Everest and be the same person,' she says.

Piya saw first-hand the political oppression in Tibet, the complete opposite of democracy. Since they crossed overland from Nepal instead of flying in like most tourists do, they stood in queues with returning refugees for hours and saw what it is like for the locals who live under Chinese rule. 'Freedom is something we take for granted. In Tibet, there are restrictions on everything. Even toilet breaks on the road were determined by rules. These are the experiences that are humbling, life-changing. No retelling or writing can truly convey what you feel when you stand in a line like that.'

She returned to Mumbai charged with a passion to see new places, share what she had experienced and help others travel to their dream destinations. Before she had left, she had toyed with the idea of taking up a job in the field of intellectual property law, a subject she had enjoyed in college, but the trip had helped her make one decision—she wanted to live rather than just earn a living. 'By the time I returned to India, I was more aware and had learnt to be thankful for whatever I had. That gave me the confidence to start Girls on the Go with practically nothing but confidence.'

Travel helps her see the ordinary and the everyday with new appreciation. 'To me, travelling is meditation. It may merely be the act of getting out of my ordinary life to go halfway around the world to see other people living their ordinary lives, but this is the one thing that gives me unadulterated joy.'

She considered a career as a travel writer, but the question of how to get more Indian women to travel without their families was always at the back of her mind. More women were working and had the desire and the income to see the world, but safety was the reason why they either hesitated or were forbidden to travel alone. It bothered her that one of the most liberating experiences was off limits to Indian women simply because they could not pack up and head out on their own.

The age-old idea of safety in numbers came to her in a flash as the answer. Why not bring these many aspiring solo travellers together and do a trip? 'A travel forum solely for women would help them discover themselves through travel, just like I had found my calling after a month on the road,' says Piya. An all-women's forum would also free them from the typical family holiday responsibilities of caring for husbands and children, and allow them to let their hair down completely.

Her family thought she was crazy. They pointed out the fact that she had no savings and therefore no capital, and no chance of raising a loan since she had no job or business experience. Her father was especially disappointed and critical, and insisted that she find another job in the legal field even if not in a law firm. Friends from abroad seemed to be more understanding, and she took courage from her Couchsurfing visitors who shared their stories of giving up houses, jobs, cars and more just to follow their dreams.

In June 2008, Piya announced a ten-day, all-women's trip to Ladakh. She had no idea how to plan a trip for a group, but she did a lot of research and drew up an itinerary. Piya chose Ladakh because she was just back from high-altitude Tibet. 'I was aware of the kinds of problems altitude and cold throw at you and felt I could tackle it.'

Long before harnessing the power of social media marketing was a given, Piya wrote to women on Orkut—the most popular social networking site in India before Facebook caught on—explaining that she was a lawyer looking to lead a travel group to Ladakh. She sent announcements to newspapers and magazines that had free listing sections. 'Honestly, I did not expect a single sign-up. But call it beginner's luck, in one month, twenty-five women signed up for my first trip.' The girls were all set to go.

The trip was scheduled for August, so Piya began booking tickets, making reservations and figuring out how to deal with local tour operators in Ladakh. A week before the group was scheduled to reach Srinagar, riots broke out and all flights were cancelled. She gave people the option of backing out because rebooking flights from Delhi to Leh meant having to spend Rs 5000 more. 'No one did. Meeting the whole group at the Delhi airport was one of the happiest moments of my life,' she says.

For many of the women, it was their first trip without family. 'We were quite a sight—women from the ages of eighteen to sixty having so much fun, feeling so free. We got our fair share of attention in Manali and Leh,' she says, laughing.

At Sarchu, where the group had stopped for the night on the drive back from Leh to Manali, a gruelling twenty-four-hour road trip traversing some of the most dramatic and stunning landscapes in the world, it started snowing heavily and the strong winds carried snow into the tents. 'It was so cold. The water was frozen. I was sure people were going to be very angry because they were way out of their comfort zone. But when I stepped out, fearing the worst, I saw the women dancing in the snow. The next morning some of them hugged me and said they had never seen or experienced anything so beautiful. The women from that first group are still friends.'

Piya knew Ladakh would be a difficult destination because of the altitude and climate, but she was obsessed with the landscape of barren mountains. 'Unless I was excited about the trip, how could I convince others to sign on?' she says. Her first international trip was to Egypt in 2009, another learning experience because she had to deal with everyone from tour operators to aggressive hawkers with a firm hand to keep the group safe and happy. To this day, Piya doesn't plan trips that don't excite her, even though her company has grown enough for her to send representatives out to lead trips.

When she decides not to lead a trip, she takes on volunteers. She chooses a person who has travelled with her before or someone who she feels resonates with her views on travel and asks that woman to lead a group in exchange for a discount on the price of the trip. Since Piya has already worked out all arrangements down to the last detail with the ground operator at the destination, there isn't too much for the group leader to do. 'The group leader just has to be the point of contact for the local handler as well as for the group to consult and coordinate with. I sometimes select a leader from within the group, someone who I feel is passionate about travel and has the potential to inspire co-travellers,' she says.

Piya experimented with the idea of another person leading the travel group in 2012 on a trip to the Andamans, when she requested a woman who had not only travelled with Girls on the Go a couple of times but was also a travel blogger to lead the group. Feedback from that first experiment was positive and, since then, Piya has found it the most effective and efficient way to handle the growing number of trips every year. She still heads out with groups to the more remote destinations, like an upcoming trip to Mongolia that she is planning.

Despite the fun she was having organizing trips, Piya hit a low point in 2013 and, for a fleeting moment, considered going back to the legal world. She had spent fourteen days with a group where a particularly fussy customer had attacked her and her work at every opportunity. She returned home physically and mentally drained. 'Sometimes in your career you come across people who are a juggernaut of negativity, and that affects you no matter how optimistic you are,' she says. 'It hurt me that no matter how passionate I was about my job, some clients would just see me as a hard-core tour operator, just because there was money involved in our equation.'

Doubt dragged her down: Should she have stayed at her corporate job, which, despite the graveyard shifts and robotic lifestyle, would have guaranteed a great salary, a fancy car and a house? Was she just a 'tour operator', a 'service provider' and nothing else? For the first time in her life she felt her love for travel drain out of her as the nuts and bolts of the business of organizing tours consumed her. 'It was the scariest feeling, not knowing whether I would ever get that zeal back,' she says.

When her father heard about the trip and the doubt in her voice, he decided it was time for her to return to law and said he would get in touch with some friends in legal circles to help her get a job. 'I was so blank that I just said yes. As soon as I put down the phone, the horror of what I had just agreed to hit me like a whip,' she says. 'I couldn't sleep that night because it all felt wrong.' She called him back and told him that she had come too far to give it all up. Obviously, an argument followed, but in her mind she was clearer than ever before that she needed to stay the course.

The next morning she found an invitation in her inbox asking her to give a talk at a local TEDx event. 'In my dazed state, I thought it was some college event,' she says. It was not till she had finished speaking from the heart to a rapt audience of entrepreneurs and MBA students about the highs and lows of starting and sustaining a zero-cash business model that she realized TED is an international forum for the exchange of innovative ideas. 'There were other speakers there who had done far more daring things than me. They all just had faith in themselves. Giving that talk and just being on that platform recharged me.'

Her father has come around since, but still says she should keep in touch with law and probably return to it when she's older. 'While I do plan to stay in touch with law as a subject of study, I don't see myself ever giving up what I have created and going back to a career in law.'

In the last couple of years, more boutique and experiential travel companies and all-women groups similar to hers have entered the market. To differentiate herself from the rest, she has started diversifying into specialized trips, such as ones themed on the Jaipur Literature Festival for book lovers, Nagaland's Hornbill festival, or expedition cruises to Antarctica and the Arctic region.

Piya handcrafts each trip, planning each one with new activities, even if the destination has been offered by her group before. For instance, her trip to Ladakh has evolved over the years and no longer just covers trips to monasteries and drives up to the Khardung-La pass and Alchi. 'Everyone does that now,' she says. Her extras are a night's stay in tents at Pangong Lake and a stop at Turtuk on the Indo-Pak border, where the landscape is even more dramatic and striking than the rest of Ladakh and the people speak Balti. 'My trip to Ladakh would probably cost about Rs 7000 more than the average operator, but the experience I offer is very different, it's off the beaten track,' she says.

Each trip takes about two months of planning and about twenty trips are conducted a year. The prices depend on the destination, starting from about Rs 15,000 for a short trip and going up to Rs 80,000 for longer ones or international destinations. The more specialized trips like the Antarctica expedition took a year of planning and promotion.

The itineraries feature activities that women might particularly enjoy such as spa treatments, shopping time and cooking classes though she's sure to include unusual experiences too such as traditional pottery classes in Madhya Pradesh and boating on the Mekong in Vietnam. 'These women are not travelling just to see new places, they also want to make friends and have fun away from their families who consume a large part of their time even on vacations. They don't have to look out for anyone but themselves and that is so liberating,' she says.

Learning the ropes in a closed, rather cut-throat business where overcharging is the norm has been a challenge, especially since she had no one to guide her. 'I have picked up everything just by doing. The praise is all mine and so are the liabilities. What makes this exciting is that you don't see a problem as a problem and grumble. You see it as a challenge and overcome it using your wit and common sense and enjoy doing this,' she says.

The women sometimes being harsh critics has helped Piya. 'They are very demanding, but I have realized that as long as their criticism is not below the belt I should be glad for it because it's made me step up my game.'

Her law training too comes in handy. 'I am glad I studied the law and worked in the unforgiving corporate legal sector. It trained me to work hard and spot flaws instantly. Those five years of legal training to think in an organized and accurate way stays with you for life.'

Girls on the Go broke even at the end of the first year and now makes a profit of about 20 per cent to 30 per cent a trip. Her main expenses are phone and Internet bills since she is sure she does not want to be tied down to an office again. In the last couple of years, she has hired freelancers to help her with marketing, database management and daily operations.

Piya is now trying to figure out how to scale up without compromising on individuality. Though some of her competitors who started around the same time have scaled up aggressively, Piya is still happy to cater to a smaller, niche segment of discerning travellers who resonate with her personal philosophy on travel. 'I don't want to grow into a huge, impersonal company, because Girls on the Go was born out of passion and I don't want to turn it into a factory. My next challenge is scaling up without losing our core philosophy or the personal touch.'

Girls on the Go has also changed the way Piya travels. When she decided to quit her corporate legal career, not knowing what to do, she started travelling to escape from her problems, worries and confusion. But somewhere down the line, as her dreams crystallized and her ideas started taking shape, she has started travelling not to escape, but to arrive.

PIYA'S TIPS FOR THE
ENTREPRENEURSHIP JOURNEY

1. The day I quit my job as a lawyer I realized I had to make certain lifestyle changes—cut down on fine dining, take the bus rather than a cab, walk more. I did not have the luxury of money, but I did have the luxury of time. I loved Mumbai and finally had more time to enjoy it. You can live life king-size at any rung of the ladder.

2. Money is not the only form of capital. Don't worry about raising financial capital. You can start most ventures without much cash, but you do need entrepreneurship, commitment and passion to give shape to your dreams.

3. Be 100 per cent honest with your clients. Don't defend a mistake. If a service you provided doesn't meet expectations, tell them you're wrong. It's important to be humble.

DRIFTING WITH A PURPOSE

Nishant Singh

Nishant Singh left an eight-year career in marketing to start a backpacking hostel in Manali, combining his passion for meeting new, interesting people every day, his childhood dream of being in the hospitality business and his desire to live a simpler life in the hills. He is now on the second leg of his journey, setting up a boutique hotel near Nainital.

Nishant Singh is, to put it his way, 'f***ing pissed'. He's spent the last thirty minutes in a bathroom, checking a pipe for a non-existent leak. Now, sitting in a spot of sunshine on the steps of his guest house, Drifters' Inn & Café in Manali, he's smoking a cigarette, watching two of his staff play badminton, and letting off steam.

A guest from Jaipur has posted a rather nasty review of Drifters' Inn online, saying the washbasin pipe in their room leaked and that their Pajero couldn't get up the road. 'They didn't mention it while they were here. There is no leak, I checked. People have stayed in the room after them without complaints. Tempo travellers and earth movers come up this road,' he says, gesturing to Old Manali Road, halfway up which his cafe and ten-room guest house sits. 'If the criticism was justified, I'd take it. I'm finicky about who stays here.'

Nishant is aware that he sounds—and looks—like a tantrum-throwing Robbie Williams complete with the sardonic twist to the mouth, edgy energy and self-assured impishness. 'Yes, it's partly to do with my ego, but that comes in because running Drifters isn't just a job to me,' he says, thumbing through his Blackberry messages to display the offending review. It's on travel portal TripAdvisor, where Drifters' Inn & Café has won the Traveller's Choice Award for two years running, 2011 and 2012, and received a Certificate of Excellence in 2012, 2013 and 2014.

For a guest house like Nishant's, traditional avenues like advertising and tying up with travel agents don't work—his guests are usually the kinds who like to do their own research and plan their itineraries, which is why online ratings and reviews are crucial. Drifters' is rated among the best places to stay in Manali on a host of travel websites, and guest after guest has left glowing reviews about the location, hospitality and Nishant himself.

The reviews aren't overblown, which is why Nishant's irritation is justified. The rooms are spotless, though basic, the staff courteous and helpful, and the food excellent. Nishant's ability to make friends easily as well as manage people with flair are personality traits suited to the hospitality business, where getting along with everyone, yet being able to lay down the law are equally important.

A couple of porters carrying stones nod acknowledgement as they pass. Someone stops by to ask if his Internet's back up after the recent flash flood. 'That's why I moved here,' he says, good humour restored. 'Mountain folk are almost always smiling. There's less stress. Plus, beautiful views are always around the corner.'

Nishant's an efficient MBA grad who grew up in Ghaziabad and spent close to eight years as a sales and brand manager in some of the country's tougher markets selling, by turn, health-care products, hair oil and edible oil, and marketing mobile services. Seven years ago, he moved to Manali and set up Drifters' Inn & Café because he wanted a simpler life. 'I'd always felt happiest in the mountains, at peace, and for as long as I could remember I'd wanted to be in the hospitality business,' says the thirty-six-year-old.

One of the waiters beckons and Nishant walks inside to settle bills with a guest who's checking out. The homely sound and smell of a cooker steaming basmati rice wafts into the cafe and blends with the 1960s rock 'n' roll playing in the background. Six Europeans play a game of Risk at a glass-topped table in a corner, plotting world domination in the unlikely war zone of green-grey mountains, snowy peaks and apple orchards.

He might have retired to the hills, but Nishant has his eye on the dice—it's just that he isn't exactly chasing what everyone else is. 'Mine is a typical UP [Uttar Pradesh], middle class, business, joint family. They're in the transportation business. It's a pretty dirty business with *ma–behen gaaliya*s [abusive language], though it pays our bills comfortably. I didn't like that atmosphere and wanted to do something different. I was the smart kid who wanted to study, and my parents encouraged me,' says Nishant, who studied in St George's College in Mussoorie from classes six to twelve.

'I loved boarding school. The atmosphere was calm, organized, so far removed from the madness of Ghaziabad and the family,' he says. Despite studying in the Hindi medium up to class five, he quickly caught up and by the eighth standard was a class prefect, an honour he held on to till he finished school as the best outgoing student in 1996.

He wanted to join catering college, but his family told him there was neither money nor a future in waiting on people. 'So I did what everyone else was doing though I didn't particularly enjoy it,' he says. After graduating first class from Shri Ram College of Commerce in Delhi, Nishant went to MDI in Gurgaon in 1999 for an MBA.

The management degree sent him back to hostel life, which he enjoyed. 'I made good friends and the classes were good. Most of what you learn during an MBA is common sense, things you can apply every day of your life,' he says. He approached human resource theory not just as employee relations, but as a means to learn how to handle people and relationships. Finance lessons weren't just for sound business planning, but a way to ensure he handled money better.

While he enjoyed the lessons and atmosphere of business school, he didn't see the point of the aggressive competiveness. 'I had good scores, but never fared well in group discussions. I would see people shouting gibberish just to be heard over the next guy. So I would sit silently rather than talk nonsense,' says Nishant.

Since he wouldn't shout with the crowd, during campus placements he only got picked on Day 2 by Dabur at a starting salary lower than most of what his classmates signed up for. 'A lot of people got great jobs just by being loud. My friends were upset I didn't sign for a large sum like the rest of them. I was okay with it though. I had a job and could always move up from there,' he says. 'I'm still like that; I don't belong with the *janta*. I carve the world I want around me, a world of my choosing, and I live within that, being completely myself.'

After a year and a half of handling sales of health-care products in Nagpur for Dabur, Nishant interviewed for a sales manager's job with Marico in December 2002. Marico are the makers of, most famously, Parachute coconut oil. 'The two posts available were for Chhattisgarh, based out of Raipur, and for West Bengal and Sikkim, based out of Kolkata. Obviously, I wanted West Bengal and Sikkim because it was close to the mountains,' he says. But the sales and development head of Marico wasn't convinced that a boy from Ghaziabad, with only a year's experience, was the right man. 'The company's market share was dropping there. They wanted someone with more than three years' experience, not me.'

As expected, being told he couldn't do something made him want to prove himself. 'That's what I mean by saying I define my own competition. I wanted that job all the more because Marico is an extremely professional organization, and West Bengal was tough territory and a challenge. It would give me a chance to prove my abilities and also travel to the mountains. My body language changed at that point and I became more assertive saying I would take the job as a personal challenge. I got three months to sort out the mess. I sorted out the mess.'

Becoming the regional star performer of the year and changing the brand's perception there included breaking the language barrier, putting new systems in place, firing non-performers, and facing angry distributors. 'All sorts of crazy things happened, but all of it honed my leadership skills. I was on a high,' he says.

Holidays and the time between sales calls were spent travelling in the eastern Himalayas, to Sikkim, northern

West Bengal and Bhutan. The dream of being in the hospitality business alternated with that of living and working in the mountains. On work trips and holidays, Nishant would observe the working of hotels and kitchens. After a long day at work, he'd go home, look at pictures of mountains in magazines, and imagine waking up to a view of the hills every morning.

In April 2004, he moved to Mumbai on a sales assignment, and a year later joined the Saffola brand team. He switched jobs six months later to join the brand team at telecom company Hutch. He spent three and a half years with Hutch (which later became Vodafone), working fifteen-hour days and weekends, not taking holidays or breaks. 'I joined them because I liked their customer-centric communication, and thought there would be a lot of creative work and a vibrant environment. While it was all of that, it was also extremely strenuous. There was no work–life balance. Every decimal point of market share matters in the telecom sector, so you're working all the time, sometimes not even having any time to think,' he says.

The dream of working in the hospitality business and the hills was forgotten. Instead, as a senior brand manager, he focused on being a good leader, earning the respect of his team and performing well. 'I've always aspired to be a good leader. It's what I push myself to be,' he says. In August 2008, he was sent for a week-long training workshop in Lonavala to prepare him to take on a senior management position. 'They picked the wrong place,' laughs Nishant.

Long treks in the misty green hills made Nishant rediscover his love for the mountains. 'Looking at the hills, something happened within me. I realized how I didn't want what I had going for me. I made up my mind to quit and live in the mountains. There was no plan. I just wanted a simpler life. It's what I'd always wanted,' he says.

Back in Mumbai, he spent a month analysing his heart's decision with his practical MBA head. 'When I connected with nature after so many years, I realized how much I'd missed it. I was making a lot of money, but I wasn't proud of what I was doing with my life. I was not happy with the way I was conducting myself and the kind of decisions I had to make keeping in mind the organization's way of working. Switching companies would make no difference since I'd face the same issues of work ethics because people across organizations are the same,' says Nishant. He gave himself a month to change his mind, but each day his resolve only grew stronger.

Not earning a steady salary to support his lifestyle was his biggest fear. He considered saving up before making the move. Another fear was living alone—he was single and knew it was unlikely he'd meet someone in the mountains. 'Slowly, I realized I would never save "enough". I could wait for ever to meet "the one". You realize that all these are just excuses for you to shy away from what you really want to do,' he says. 'Finally, the desire to run away from the corporate rat race became far stronger than the fear of losing these things.'

He quit in September and began his notice period. Some people told him he was crazy, others cheered him on. His parents tried dissuading him, but gave in. 'My last day in the corporate world was 31 December 2008,' he says. 'I just wanted to move to my dream destination and do whatever it took to stay there.'

He had vague ideas about starting a day spa in Himachal Pradesh or Uttarakhand. He considered taking a teaching job in a boarding school in the hills. Finally, he decided that his first step before embarking on a new life would be to spend a few months travelling across the country.

After a month in Rajasthan, he reached Manali on 16 February 2009. 'Manali was among my first choices of places to live in because it snows here properly every year. Silly, no?' he says. It had snowed by the time he reached, drifts against doorways, inches piled on roofs, and trees delicately frosted with white. 'The first snowfall is just the most beautiful thing. Even now, I've been here seven years, I just can't get bored of it,' he says.

His plan was to spend some time in Manali and test the waters before continuing his travels. 'If I could survive here in the harshest of winters, I would probably enjoy living here the rest of the year. I loved every day I spent in Manali that winter. I never left,' he says. 'I forgot my plan to travel around the whole country.' Within a week, both his dreams coalesced neatly in his head: he would live in Old Manali and run a guest house and cafe.

Manali is a tourist town with a seasonal summer economy, so the cluster of small shops, with their playful staff calling out, 'Hello please, how are you? Come look, pretty things here,' which make the market so vibrant, begin winding up from October. Most hotel owners and staff, Ayurvedic masseurs, cab drivers, yoga teachers, dreadlock braiders, and peddlers of pashmina shawls, printed pants and other paraphernalia pack up their wares, move en masse to Goa, Pushkar, Kerala, Hampi and Gokarna to continue business. Manali becomes a virtual ghost town after October, restored to the locals who live in the villages higher up in the mountains. Business would be seasonal—from April to October—and the staff would change every year, he realized.

Since Himachal Pradesh legislation only allows local domiciles to own land, all the cramped, narrow buildings belong to landlords who live in the village farther up the winding Old Manali Road. Leases usually run only for the season, so most landlords were free and happy to chat when Nishant went knocking on doors in the middle of winter looking for a place to start working on his dream.

Talking to locals, most of whom rely on tourism for a living, helped him hone his target audience and understand the town. Manali was slowly moving up the tourist value chain, no more just a stop for marijuana-smoking hippies and tourists on a tight budget. Europeans, North Americans and upper-middle-class Indians wanting adventure sports or relaxed holidays had started heading there. Nishant saw space for the kind of cosy yet classy place he imagined, where people passionate about travelling would break journey before heading off for treks, adventure sports or the long road trip to Ladakh.

Manali in winter is grey and quiet, with no activity—depressing to most, beautiful to Nishant. 'I went for long walks; I sat and did nothing in particular. I was learning to be with myself again. I had been lost in the last few years at Hutch and Vodafone,' he says. Since it got dark early, evenings were spent in his room with his laptop, putting down thoughts, ideas, plans and what he'd learnt from the locals.

'The idea came to be this: This is my home that I am opening up to guests. The decor, design, food, rooms, ambience, service, everything has to reflect that,' says Nishant, who lives in a room on the terrace that looks up at a sky the shade of blue you only see in the mountains and, of course, snowy Himalayan peaks.

'I guess I had all the fears that anyone doing something like this would, but my willpower was far stronger and that carried me through. There was desire, passion and determination to stick by it plus—as is always in my case—ego,' he says.

No one in his world—family, friends, colleagues, friends of friends or relatives of friends—had thrown up a job and a salary to start a hotel. 'I didn't know anyone who had taken such a decision so I wanted to make it work. A lot of people buckle under the pressure. I, on the other hand, took it up as a challenge to myself,' he says, as—in an odd coincidence—'Blue Moon' wafts from the speakers, filling the gap in the conversation with the lyrics, 'Without a fear in my heart, without a love of my own.'

There wasn't much time to worry as new ideas and possibilities filled his mind. Nishant's business plan was more like a product brief, a habit carried over from his old job. 'I had to define my product, and identify the right target group and my positioning within the market. I saw a market for a budget place with good food and service.' As he's talking, the delicate drizzle outside becomes heavier and Nishant spots rain coming in through a window. He jumps up, shuts all the windows on that side, rushes to get a cloth and wipes the wooden frames dry. 'If you want guests coming in, you have to be on your toes all the time,' he says, settling back down in the chair.

Finding a willing landlord to rent to him wasn't as hard as finding the perfect building since most guest houses are run by outsiders who lease property for a season. They're used to outsiders setting up guest houses during the season and short-term leases are easy to draw up. After a few weeks of intense scouting, Nishant found the right kind of building—on the main road, a view of the mountains, ten rooms, space for a cafe, and a parking lot. He signed the lease in mid-March and started work on the nitty-gritty details.

He had a couple of lakh in the bank and provident fund dues that would arrive in a few months. He borrowed from his father to tide him over and began work on his new life. Nishant realized that most of the things he wanted had to be brought from Delhi, whether it was the comfy bamboo furniture that gives the cafe its warm feel or the fluffy white towels in the bathrooms. 'The local market doesn't have good-quality stuff. That's the downside of running a business here, but it teaches you to plan better,' says Nishant. He stocks up during his trips to Delhi in winter, when the guest house is closed for a month since the snow is too heavy for tourists from the plains.

To go with the theme of drifting, he framed photographs of famous, focused 'drifters'—Portuguese explorer Vasco da Gama, American aviator Charles Lindbergh, Italian explorer Christopher Columbus, Brazilians Diogo Guerreiro and Flávio Jardim who windsurfed the length of the coast of their country, long-distance German cyclist Heinz Stücke and several others. 'They all went where no one else had before, just for the sake of exploring. They drifted in a sense, yet had purpose,' Nishant says.

He found his eleven employees among the itinerant population that services all tourist towns. Though he wasn't a chef, he knew what would go down well with tourists looking for comfort food with an Indian touch—bacon-and-egg breakfasts till noon, and Manali trout, Goan curry, baguettes—the kind of food most tourist-town cooks can whip up. 'I had eaten at most of the places in Manali and knew what kind of food I wanted to serve. The staff I hired had a lot of experience. I learnt about stocking and sourcing from them,' he says.

By April, things were coming together so Nishant invited his family up for a visit. 'That reassured them a bit.

They saw something concrete, they stopped worrying that maybe I was just going to become a pothead,' he says. 'I learnt much later that my father had been very angry with me till that point. To his credit, he didn't let it be known to me,' he says.

Drifters' Inn opened on 6 May 2009, and the cafe on 13 May. It was a week before the first guest—an Australian backpacker—wandered in to take a room, but on the very first day Nishant made Rs 10 from someone who walked in to use the Internet. 'I was thrilled. In the past, my salary would always get credited to my bank account, so it was a new feeling to get those ten rupees in my hand, my first ever. I have never had to look back,' he says, a childish grin on his face as he recalls the moment.

Nishant says he doesn't look at his finances in terms of profitability so he doesn't know when exactly he broke even, though he knows he's never run at a loss. 'My business planning has been to ensure perfection in the guest experience. I don't take a salary, I don't have many expenses since I live here. Whatever I make goes back into the business, with enough set aside, in case we have a slow month and to build savings,' he says. Nishant has a clear count of how many guests have to come to the cafe and the inn to ensure he can pay salaries, buy stocks and keep himself in rajma and rice, his favourite food. 'It is a business because it has to sustain itself—which it does—but I don't measure its success solely in terms of profitability.'

The competition is fierce in a place like Manali where guest houses and homestays cling to every rock face. To ensure that his trusted staff stays with him, Nishant pays them during the off season too, a rare practice in the town. 'If you want people to stay with you, take care of them,' he says. 'Now, the guys go home and spend time with their families during the off season instead of running to Goa to work some more. They come back well-rested and happy when we open again in February–March after the snow melts.'

The real differentiator between Drifters' and the many other guest houses is the fact that Manali is home to Nishant, not a place to do summer business as it is to most of the guest-house operators. 'Except for one month in winter when I go home to Ghaziabad to see my family, I live here full-time. Guests are literally coming into my home,' he says.

The ten rooms, priced between Rs 800 and Rs 2000, are usually full, and the cafe has its share of drifters all day. Evenings are usually packed with people coming in not only for the delicious food but also the open mic sessions and music nights. He makes it a point to chat with most guests in the cafe, and those who stay, he knows by name. 'It is designed and run like a place that I would want to return to because it is the place I live in. That's the approach I'd take to any property I open.'

Drifters' Inn and Café turned five in May 2014, and though he hasn't tired of the view, he isn't settling too comfortably into an armchair either. Nishant's started work on creating a new eight-room boutique hotel in Mukteshwar, about 45 km from Nainital in Uttarakhand.

'Having achieved the Manali dream, I thought of taking on another challenge and creating something new from scratch—yet again,' he says. Drifters' still requires his attention, but the routine has been set, the staff knows their jobs, the crowds are coming in—and Nishant knows it's time to look for inspiration again. 'Drifters' has done far, far better than I expected, but it's reached its high point and I don't want it or myself to stagnate. It's good to take a dream further, to plan again, to challenge myself again,' he says.

This time, he's moving up the value chain and has chosen his location with even greater care—among rolling hills with beautiful views and an abundance of bird and animal life. The Birdcage, as the hotel is named because the place is filled with birdsong, is a seven-hour drive from Delhi. 'It's easier to plan a weekend getaway from Delhi because the driving distance is shorter and the roads are better. Even people coming from Bangalore or Mumbai can fly to Delhi first and then take buses, taxis or trains from there to Kathgodam. Manali is a little harder to access in that sense,' he says. Manali does not have direct train links; the drive from Delhi is about sixteen hours, and it has been getting rather crowded and chaotic in the last couple of years.

In 2013, Nishant used his savings from Drifters' to buy the land on which the Birdcage is coming up, solving the issue of having to renew his lease every year. Uttarakhand, unlike Himachal Pradesh, allows outsiders to own land. 'I now know how the hospitality business runs and that it is better to do it on your own terms, especially for someone like me who is not just chasing seasonal tourists,' he says. 'One of my primary aims is to live here and enjoy the peace of the hills.'

Manali is more backpacker country with travellers looking for clean rooms, good food and music and nightlife. In Mukteshwar, the focus will be on conscientious service, good food and indulgent relaxation—much of the experience will revolve around just lazing and gazing.

Construction of the property began in May 2014, leading to Nishant's learning curve peaking again. 'Just procuring land and planning the funding was an experience. The best part has been getting a feel of architecture and engineering— meeting the architect, designing the place, finding the right contractor, understanding what construction materials to use . . . so much to learn,' he says.

'A lot of what is going into the design of the Birdcage is based on what I've learnt from my guests here at Drifters'. Many of my guests are happy backpacking to Manali and around, but they can easily afford special breaks where they are willing to spend more just to relax,' he says.

The plan is to create a high-end mountain lodge for more discerning guests looking for a relaxing break from their hectic work lives. His target is the slightly evolved traveller who wants a calm, luxurious environment to recuperate from urban life and reconnect with family and with nature, who wants to go on nature walks and birdwatching, or spend time in the spa.

'Drifters' has taught me a lot about what a discerning traveller requires. I've figured out small things like where you need electrical sockets to charge your devices—near a window with a view, not just by the bed, what kind of armchairs are more comfy, things like that. All these little lessons are going into the Birdcage,' he says. 'I have more control over everything since I am building it. At Drifters' I had to work within the existing building.'

The Kumaon region of Uttarakhand will become his new home by early 2017 after Drifters' is closed by the end of 2016. 'It seems like a natural transition. I don't want to be an absentee owner, so, as much as I love Drifters', I will close it down,' he says.

He's introducing the Birdcage to his current guests and hoping some of them will become regulars there. Those of the staff who want to relocate to Uttarakhand will also go with him, but they'll make the decision a little later on. One person who will be moving with him for sure is his partner of just over two years with whom he lives and works. 'We met and clicked,' says Nishant, not really wanting to elaborate.

After seven years in the hospitality business and the hills, Nishant knows he can never return to his old life in the city. 'I wanted a lifestyle change, a simpler, more meaningful life where I made a difference to the few lives that I came in contact with. I wanted to enjoy what I do, not just do what others wanted me to or what everybody else was doing. Drifters' has given me everything I dreamt of and more,' he says.

The next challenge is setting up his new home, creating a new brand and getting people to stay with him. 'I don't want to call it Drifters' again because I want to go through the experience of creating yet another brand . . . hopefully, a successful one.'

NISHANT ON DOING WHAT ONE LOVES

1. There is no 'right time' to break away and do your own thing. You will never save enough, learn enough or be ready. Instead, just go for it. Once you decide to take the plunge, things will fall into place.
2. It's all about a lifestyle change. So adjust your lifestyle to match your new circumstances. You will earn less but you will also find that you need far less.
3. When you are your own boss and if you do well, share the credit with your team. If things go wrong, it's entirely your fault.

THE MASTER'S WAY

Kanishka Sharma

A few years into a career in sales and marketing, Kanishka Sharma decided to pursue his childhood dream of learning kung fu at the famed Shaolin temple in China. Today, the martial arts master is building his own centre, has scores of students around the world and trains armed forces, special forces as well as film stars.

There's little to distinguish the single-storeyed bungalow on a quiet residential street in Noida from the ones next to it. Bougainvillea curls over the walls and the black gate keeps out curious stares. Inside though, the lawn has been replaced with thick training mats on which six men practise kicks under the eagle eye of Shifu Kanishka Sharma, the first Indian to have trained at the Shaolin Temple Secular Disciples' Union in central China's Henan province, considered the birthplace of kung fu and Chan Buddhism.

'Completely different from where we met last time, isn't it?' says the former marketing executive who is a Shaolin warrior and a close-combat expert who trains national security and counter-terror forces. He is also an action-sequence choreographer for Bollywood, and his credits include films such as *Don* (2006), when he trained Shah Rukh Khan, Arjun Rampal and Priyanka Chopra, the 2011 Abhishek Bachchan-starrer *Game*, and *Gulab Gang* (2014), for which Madhuri Dixit trained with him for three months.

The first time we met, Kanishka and his wife Dipika, who has been his manager and business partner since they got married in 2008, were building a Shaolin temple in Malavli, a hill station about 55 km from Pune, in association with a local non-governmental organisation (NGO). Kanishka was working on his dream project—to bring the same rigour of training underpinned by a philosophy of non-violence and to spread kung fu in India. The idea was to train underprivileged students for free while taking in paying students to subsidise the cost.

The temple, set on a slope, was a jagged structure of protruding iron rods and bamboo poles, unfinished blocks and cement slabs, but the grand plan was firmly in place. A fifteen-foot Sakyamuni Buddha statue gazed down on visitors who rattled their way up the winding, potted road. A bulbous foundation stone with Chinese lettering spelling out 'Shaolin Temple India' sat in the undergrowth where two of Kanishka's masters from China had laid it in May 2012. Free Shaolin kung fu classes had started for the first batch of nine students from the NGO.

The setting was very similar to the centuries-old original in which Kanishka trained—green hills, waterfalls in the distance, the second-century Bhaja Buddhist caves a few kilometres away, and an overwhelming sense of tranquillity.

'It seemed too perfect and it was,' says Kanishka, dressed as always in a Shaolin master's orange robes over loose black trousers and Luohan cloth sandals. He has close-cropped hair, a tiny diamond stud in his left ear, and a bracelet-sized circle of beads that he fiddles with as he talks.

Less than a year in, Dipika and Kanishka realized that the NGO they were partnering with was siphoning off funds and not providing enough food and facilities to the children they had taken in. 'They lied to us. I could not come to terms with the fact that the children were being ill-treated. The land was the NGO's and even though we had invested in the construction, I decided to end that partnership immediately,' he says. Kanishka, Dipika and their son Kabir, who had moved to Pune just to build the temple, decided to return home to Noida where he could focus on his training of special forces.

'I was very disillusioned. I'm still disappointed, but I haven't lost hope of building a temple some day. It will take time, but it will happen. Shaolin kung fu teaches you that,' he says, stirring sugar into tea his mother has set down on the table. Kanishka's own ascent to Shifu, as Shaolin kung fu masters are known, has taken time and tenacity.

'I was born in Lucknow in 1977 and grew up in Delhi. My father was a journalist. Five generations of my family have been journalists and so dinner-time talk was always of politics, history and current affairs but I was just not interested,' he says. 'I loved watching kung fu movies. That's all I was interested in.'

The family's driver Suraj got the young Kanishka hooked to martial arts, and taught him moves from films. 'Suraj told me the stories of kung fu movies the way most children are told *Amar Chitra Katha* stories.' When Kanishka was about eight, Suraj brought home a video cassette of

The 36th Chamber of Shaolin, considered one of the finest kung fu films ever made. 'That was it. I wanted to be like that.'

Pester power exhausted his mother into paying for Japanese Okinawan karate classes, and about a year later, for the only kung fu classes in Delhi. 'So Monday-Wednesday-Friday, I learnt kung fu; Tuesday-Thursday-Saturday, I went for karate; plus I would practise at home. This was odd for my family,' he says.

Kanishka's father, Udayan Sharma, was a well-known editor and an advisor to former prime minister Rajiv Gandhi; his mother was a television producer; his older brother was set on becoming a journalist. 'And then there was me, kicking and screaming all the time,' he says.

Despite their worries about his total indifference to school, his parents didn't tell him to cut back on practice. 'My father only said that he expected me to pass class twelve, which I did and joined BCom (Hons) like all my friends,' he says. During this time he started training in kung fu to'a, an Iranian style of kung fu, and kalaripayattu, the Kerala martial arts form. At home, in college, at family functions and career fairs, people would ask him what he wanted to become and his answer was the seemingly unrealistic 'martial arts expert'.

'I kept pestering my parents to let me go to the Shaolin temple after college but they were not for it. They understood my love for martial arts but did not see a future in it,' he says. Instead, Kanishka was sent to Maastricht School of Management in the Netherlands for an MBA in 1999. There too, he managed to find a kung fu class, a ninety-minute train ride from the university.

Kanishka is an expert in ten martial arts forms, including Shaolin kung fu, pekiti-tirsia kali Filipino blade fighting, kung fu to'a, jeet kune do, kalaripayattu, Muay

Thai and tai chi, but can't explain what it is about them that attracts him. 'I don't know. I'm just a different person when I'm training or teaching. I come alive,' he says.

Dipika says Kanishka transforms when he's studying, practising or teaching. 'His great passion for the martial arts is quite clear. He may not impress in a room full of people talking politics or current affairs, he gets bored and you can see it. But, with his students or masters, he's 100 per cent happy,' she says. 'It's his first love.'

Back in Delhi after the year-long MBA, Kanishka joined Reliance Industries's plastics and petrochemicals division as a sales and marketing manager. 'Imagine my frustration: I did not like marketing. I hated chemistry. And I had a job that combined the two,' he says. At twenty-three, he was in charge of marketing products to 350 dealers in north India. 'It might have been exciting for someone else. I felt like a glorified clerk. It was the most depressing period of my life.'

He'd been learning martial arts for twelve years by then, and started teaching kung fu to'a in Noida to counter the frustration. 'The real, serious teaching began only after I came back from China; that's when I made the decision to give my life to martial arts,' he says. While most martial arts instructors charged Rs 300 a month, Kanishka's fee was Rs 700. 'I knew I was better than the others,' he says, laughing at his confidence.

Colleagues at Reliance sent their children for lessons, and slowly the classes picked up. He would start his own training at 4 a.m., be at work from 9 a.m. to 5 p.m., and then head to Noida to teach. 'It was more frustrating because work would run late and my classes would get delayed. Soon I learnt a trick of the trade,' Kanishka says. He would do all his paperwork in the morning and tell his boss he was out on field visits in the afternoon. 'I'd wind up visits to the plastic market early and head to the gym by three-thirty or four,' he says. 'Not right, I know, but I felt so stifled by the job.'

He started looking for a way out, and visited the Chinese embassy to find out about studying at the Shaolin temple. 'By this time, my father had been diagnosed with cancer and was very sick. We had long talks. He told me there was no point working for Reliance if I was so uninterested. "You cannot love everything you do, but if you are doing something, give it 100 per cent, otherwise stop doing it," were his words,' says Kanishka. His father died in March 2001. Kanishka resigned from his job in April.

When he told his mother Neelima, she was extremely upset since money was tight after the expenses of her husband's long illness, and she didn't think Kanishka could live off kung fu. 'It was a tough decision to leave my mother after my father's death, but I knew I had to go,' he says.

Travelling to China wasn't simple in 2001, and talking to embassy staff, Kanishka realized he was the first Indian trying to get to the temple where warriors are made. He got a two-month tourist visa in May 2001, and booked a ticket to Shanghai, a connecting flight to Zhengzhou in Henan province, and found a bus that would take him to Dengfeng, where the Shaolin temple is located at the base of the Songshan mountain. 'Today, there is an expressway, and you get there in an hour. Back then it was a slow journey,' he says. It was a journey made longer by the fear of what lay ahead combined with the itchy excitement of the promise of a dream coming true.

Delhi-boy Kanishka, used to wide roads, bright lights and honking traffic, found himself in the middle of a Chinese village full of kung fu fighters. 'You feel like you are in a different era. Dengfeng has hundreds of kung fu

schools. The way you see farmers in the fields here, you see
people practising kung fu there. Swords are flashing on one
side, people are jumping, kicking, everyone is shouting the
commands. It is an unbelievable sight,' he says.

'Then I saw the gates of the Shaolin temple. I had tears
in my eyes. Standing in front of the Shaolin temple for the
first time, the feeling is indescribable. I thought: "I'm here.
This is everything I wanted in life." That's a rare feeling and
so wonderful. Nothing has matched it ever since.'

Humility was a lesson he learnt on the first day in the
Shaolin temple. Kanishka saw the Grand Master, Da Shifu
Shi Heng Jun, and touched his feet. He welcomed Kanishka
and said they'd start the next day. 'I was so excited that Da
Shifu, as we call the Grand Master, would be teaching me.
The next day, an eight-year-old boy was leading my class.'
After the initial shock and disappointment, Kanishka and
the twenty others in the class started training. 'The child
was excellent. The Master wanted to show us that you can
learn from anyone, and that we had to swallow whatever
big ideas we had built up about ourselves,' he says. A few
weeks later, after the edge had been knocked off them, a
senior instructor took over the class.

It wasn't just his views he had to change; there was the
language, food, culture and everything else to adjust to as
well. A student from Hong Kong with perfect Chinese and
imperfect English helped him communicate. 'At first you
don't eat because the food is terrible, but if you don't eat,
you don't have energy to train for eight hours. It's quite a
hostile place and they don't like to share their knowledge
easily, especially with foreigners. You really have to prove
your mettle to be accepted.'

Training started at 5 a.m. with the greenhorns running
1 km up the mountain and crawling back on all fours like

dogs, in twenty minutes. Breakfast at seven, classes till eleven and lunch at noon, followed by study and chores. 'We did the cleaning, cooking, washing, in rotation; things I'd never done before.' From three to six, they were out practising again. 'An hour for dinner eaten in complete silence. We'd sit in lines and focus only on the food,' he says. Eight to nine was the last hour of practice. 'That was the toughest class because I'd feel sleepy after eating.' Usually, night training was punching a candle on a table 100 times while sitting in *mabu* (squatting in a half-sitting, half-standing pose the way you'd be if you were on a horse without the animal beneath you). If the flame went out, you did twenty push-ups and started punching again from one.

After the first week, he called his mother to tell her that he was exhausted, no one understood him, the food was inedible, he had to clean toilets, the training was too hard, and he wanted to come home. 'I got no sympathy,' he says. 'She said, "It's just seven weeks, finish it." It was good advice because I slowly got used to it and started enjoying it.'

One morning, Kanishka pulled a face during practice because his body was stiff and aching. 'My *laoshi* (instructor) said something to another guy who went away. Two minutes later, I saw the guy carrying my bags out. Then the translator told me the laoshi wanted me to leave since I was not interested in learning. I didn't know what to do; he would not listen when I tried apologizing. I spent that night outside the temple and the next morning I fell at his feet and apologized again. He took me back, and I learnt another lesson.'

By mid-July, he was back in Delhi and making plans to raise the money to return. 'It cost about Rs 50,000 a month to train there,' he says. The Shaolin-return tag helped, and friends of friends in DD Bharati signed him for a twenty-six-episode series, *Synergy of Martial Arts.* 'I had never been on TV but had to direct, script and anchor a show,' he says.

Kanishka put his MBA skills to use and applied the concept of FAB (Features, Advantages, Benefits) analysis to his shows. 'I got experts in different martial arts to highlight the features, advantages and benefits of each form in a mix of theory and practice,' he says. The show, which aired towards the end of 2001, did well enough to fund his next two-month trip in September. 'I realized that there is money in television and not enough money in working in an office.'

He thought he was perfectly prepared for the second session, working out rigorously and practising what he had learnt. Except by September winter begins in central China. Temperatures fell to one degree but they continued training outdoors, this time bare-chested. A new and rather tortuous exercise was squatting in mabu and slapping the surface of cold water in barrels left outdoors overnight. 'Your hands get so numb. My teacher told me to eat raw garlic at breakfast to stay warm. It helped . . . a little.'

The idea behind the gruelling training is to use physical discomfort to strengthen the mind. Kanishka spent hours in mabu, and now, in his classes in Noida too, punishment for getting moves wrong involves squatting in the horse posture. 'If I tell you to stand in mabu for two hours, your legs start hurting and quivering in ten minutes and your mind tells you to stop. But you train your mind. You tell yourself hold on, five more minutes. Mental toughness develops. So in a crisis, you don't give up. Your mind is accustomed to fighting. That is a lesson you can apply to life. You don't succumb to pressure,' he explains.

After several such trips and a fair amount of newspaper coverage as the first Indian to train at the

Shaolin temple, he got a call from National Geographic channel. They were planning a mini-series *Seven Deadly Arts with Akshay Kumar* to go on air in mid-2004. 'I was quite thrilled. I had to train Akshay Kumar in Shaolin kung fu and other martial arts and perform with him on the show. After that, there was an enormous amount of newspaper coverage,' he says. 'My classes and seminars became very popular.'

He did another show for Doordarshan and received CNBC's Young Turk Award in 2005. He was also teaching in a number of Delhi schools and running five centres. 'I didn't realize what I was doing when I set off for the Shaolin temple. I just wanted to study there because I loved the form but the publicity really helped me. I was tagged as the person who had brought kung fu back to this country, where it is believed to have originated,' he says.

As Kanishka's skills peaked, training and exhibition videos went online and one day, out of the blue, he got a call from Angelo Sahin, who introduced himself as the action director of *Mission Impossible 2*. He'd seen Kanishka's videos online, read about him and decided to rope him in to coordinate the fight sequences for a Hindi film titled *Don*. 'I told him I'd only done television, never films but was willing to try,' says Kanishka.

Late that night, his phone rang again. This time it was Bollywood director Farhan Akhtar, who told him *Don* starred Shah Rukh Khan, Priyanka Chopra and Arjun Rampal. 'I was in some other world,' says Kanishka. 'I didn't believe it till the tickets to travel to Mumbai arrived.'

Kanishka had to meet Akhtar in Mumbai and give a demonstration before signing the contract. 'His idea was that each character should use a different martial arts style,' Kanishka says. He travelled with the team to Langkawi and

Kuala Lumpur and, when it was finally released in 2006, *Don* was a huge hit. 'Shah Rukh Khan gave interviews in which he mentioned me. Overnight, I became Shah Rukh's trainer,' he says.

Back in China though, he was still 'chotu', the nickname his Chinese instructors had given him apart from the Chinese name of Shi Yan Du, because the 5'6" Kanishka was much smaller than the average aspiring warrior. 'I trained with the instructors for three years, spending six months a year in China and the rest earning money in India to fund the study,' he says. Apart from running classes and seminars, he became a consultant for a number of high-end security companies that provided bodyguards to captains of industry.

In 2004, he went back to Dengfeng as usual for a two-month stint—the visa process never got easier—and Da Shifu Shi Heng Jun came to inspect the class. 'I would long for him to teach us at least one move but he would not even talk to us. That day he called three of us out—one guy from Greece, one guy from Spain who was a police officer, and me. He had chosen us as disciples.'

They were the only ones chosen from all the foreigners training that year, and among the ten men the Grand Master picked from 300-odd students. 'Then the real training starts—in breath control, meditation, Buddhism and the philosophy that underpins kung fu,' he says. 'Until then you learn to perfect the moves. The difference between what the instructors teach you and what the Shifu and Da Shifu teach you is like earth and sky.' The Grand Master was sent to France for a while so Kanishka trained under Shifu Shi Yan Fang.

By then, he'd done a short course at Henan University and his Chinese had improved. 'To understand the finer points, meditation and breath control, you need to know Chinese. At first, when you're just mastering the moves and training the body, you can manage with a translator,' he says.

The essence of Shaolin kung fu is not to harm. 'Though you have the power to harm or kill, you learn to be humble enough not to use it unnecessarily,' he says. The Shaolin system believes in meditation in movement, calmness in motion. 'They don't sit in a silent room and meditate. To achieve calmness in stillness is easy but to be calm in chaos, that is what kung fu teaches you,' says Kanishka. 'When you achieve calmness in motion you react perfectly. You know how they slow d-o-w-n scenes in kung fu movies,' he says, drawing out the words to illustrate the meaning, 'to show the attacking kick and then speed it up at the point where the hero blocks it? That's become a gimmicky way to shoot fight scenes, but in reality when you are truly calm and fighting in the Shaolin way, every move of the opponent comes at you s-l-o-w-l-y.' Then he tones it down to a more everyday example: When you're driving and someone cuts dangerously close, there is no alarm, no quickening of the heart, no fear. All extra sounds fade out and the action seems to slow. 'So I react better with control, without panic. That's meditation in motion,' he says.

Back at the training session, Kanishka straightens a shoulder here, an arm or a palm there, explains how those tiny changes can make all the difference while warding off an attack. Then it's time for the master class: two of the senior students stomp, jump and kick exceptionally but it's not good enough for Kanishka who demonstrates. The difference is immense. There's greater ease, grace, speed and precision and a sense of weightlessness when the Shifu twirls, whirls, kicks and attacks.

Training here is far less rigorous than at the Shaolin temple in China. 'You can't be as tough here, I've learnt. People drop out if the training is intense so I use fewer punishments, very little mabu time,' he says. At his house, he trains small groups of the more serious students from his corporate classes, martial arts teachers looking to perfect their skills, and police or private security guards who have signed up out of interest. His instructors lead regular sessions in corporate houses in Noida and Gurgaon, while short-term courses for children, women and thrill-seekers are tailored as an introduction to self-defence and the basic philosophy of kung fu. Masters from the Shaolin temple in China make regular visits not only to run training programmes but also to check on what Kanishka is doing.

'They come to check that the courses are not too commercialized, that the spirit of Shaolin kung fu is being imparted,' says Dipika, who came up with the plan for introductory courses to draw in people.

They've just bought about two acres of land in Pangot near Nainital in Uttarakhand and have started the process of setting up a centre again. This time, they are being a little less ambitious and will only be putting up a dormitory for poorer students, luxury tent accommodation for paying guests, and a training centre. They plan to run a range of short-term courses that combine kung fu with trekking as Pangot is a popular birdwatchers' destination. 'If people like the short courses, they can sign on for the longer ones that run to a couple of months. We're moving slowly this time and we'll take care of all the expenses and planning by ourselves,' says Dipika.

The free and subsidised classes continue in Noida, and the Uttarakhand centre will initially function as a place for people to get a feel for kung fu's principles. The dorms will open up later with residential facilities for students who can't pay the full fee yet want to take up martial arts as a career. 'That's something I want people to realize—that they can make a living from martial arts just like they do in any other career,' he says.

Kanishka and Dipika run two companies—Shaolin Temple India, which focuses on Shaolin kung fu, and Pekiti-Tirsia Kali India to popularize the close-combat Filipino blade-fighting system that Kanishka is a master of as well.

Kanishka went to the Philippines to train in kali in 2008, after the Mumbai terror attacks when he read about how underprepared the Indian security forces were. 'The attacks happened on our wedding day,' says Dipika. 'We were watching the news after the wedding. Kanishka felt awful that our forces didn't have the skills needed to save their own lives. He felt helpless. I realized that he needed to do something about it, not like the rest of us who felt outrage or sadness and then let it be.'

Kanishka had been introduced to kali while learning jeet kune do in Bangkok in 2004 and was convinced it was the best form of offence and defence for the police and armed forces. So he set off for the Philippines immediately to learn it, again the first Indian to train and master the deadly form. The close-combat blade-fighting system has for long been part of the regular training for elite and special armed forces and commandos in the US, UK, France and Germany, and has recently gained mainstream attention after it was used in stunts in the *Bourne* film trilogy.

Kanishka was back in the field, following a punishing schedule, and this time learning to kill in three seconds. Training for kali is rigorous, aggressive and lonely, as the individual has to be transformed into a ruthless fighter. This time too his drive and focus impressed, and he found himself advancing through the ranks faster than the rest and is now two ranks below grandmaster.

Shaolin kung fu and kali are diametrically opposite in philosophy and approach. While kung fu is about being calm and controlled, kali is cut-throat and brutal. Shaolin kung fu's driving principle is to defend and defeat, kali's is to attack and kill. Kanishka needed to reorient his outlook to learn that he would have to kill or be killed.

'Looking back, I don't know how I survived the training. You train by yourself in harsh conditions for more than nine hours a day without a break, unlike the Shaolin temple where there are fighters all around you, learning with you. Parts of the kali training and test were horrifying. You learn to be cold, brutal, ruthless,' he says. 'But those skills are essential for the armed forces.'

After a couple of months, Kanishka returned and began doing the rounds of government offices. 'They were amazed by this system where you can kill someone in three seconds if you want to, but it took time for special forces and army men to accept a trainer without any kind of military background. I gave demo after demo and refused to give up. Finally, they signed me on,' he says. His first four-year government contract was to train the Indian Air Force's Garud Commando unit. More special forces signed up slowly and now instructors from Pekiti-Tirsia Kali India are placed at Special Forces Training School, Nahan, and National Security Guards (NSG) Training Headquarters, Manesar. Kanishka works with more than a dozen special forces units, police groups, counter-terror and Naxal forces and private security agencies.

Kali overshadowed all other martial arts courses after he returned from the Philippines in 2009. For the first two years, he taught every course himself. Dipika says the gruelling training and ruthless approach slowly began changing Kanishka's personality. 'He became aggressive, detached and cold, and was ignoring the kung fu classes. We discussed the change in his personality and I asked him if that was the person he wanted to be,' she says.

He stepped back a bit and started visiting his Shaolin classes, which he had left entirely to his instructors. 'I rediscovered my love for Shaolin and—in a sense—myself. Who I am is a Shaolin teacher. That is the philosophy that underpins my life,' Kanishka says. He still opens and closes all workshops and programmes he does for the armed forces but the bulk of the classes are taken by instructors he's trained.

In June 2014, Kanishka was back at the Shaolin temple in China for a ceremony to receive blessings from the abbot, Shi Yongxin, and be conferred his new name, Shi Yan You meaning The Perfect One. He has been appointed the official representative of the Shaolin Temple China in India. Kanishka has also started learning traditional Chinese medicine and hopes to practise it at his upcoming centre.

'When I first went to the Shaolin temple, I never dreamt so much—the classes, armed forces contracts and film opportunities—would come of it,' says Kanishka. 'I've been scared many times, but even on the hardest days I've never felt I made a mistake.'

KANISHKA'S ADVICE

1. In many ways, you have to revolt against your parents if you want to pursue something different. Be soft yet hard, like water which flows yet makes its own path. Be persistent but not offensive.

2. There are so many opportunities now and so much information is available easily. There is no such thing as failure, only mistakes that you learn from. If you give up, it's failure.

3. Share your knowledge to keep learning. If I share and stay open, I accumulate more knowledge, and when I share, I will feel hollow and will want to learn more.

DOING NO NASTY

Apurva Kothari

'Farmers can't really be committing suicide at that rate!' is the thought that got technology manager Apurva Kothari interested in organic produce. As he learnt that farmer suicides were indeed rising on the back of unsustainable agricultural practices, he returned to India and set up an organic and fair-trade clothing brand to create awareness about alternatives to conventional cotton.

A hand-painted cloth sign on Bandra's Hill Road in Mumbai announces 'Farmers' Market'. In the small yard are a dozen or so stalls squashed together and selling organic vegetables, homemade brownies and cinnamon rolls, cloth bags and handmade notebooks. At one stall—an arrangement of tables draped with a cloth—stands Apurva Kothari discussing farmer suicides with a person who has stopped by.

'The number of farmer suicides . . . it's just wrong,' he says. 'An average of one every half hour over fifteen years? I first read that number about six years ago. It still hasn't changed, and it still haunts me.'

It's that statistic that made the thirty-nine-year-old give up his job as a technology manager in the US and return to India to set up an organic, fair-trade clothing line in the hope of creating demand for organic cotton and eventually helping farmers make the switch from pesticide-intensive BT cultivation to more sustainable methods of farming.

Apu, as his friends call him, doesn't really fit the image of the preachy organic advocate. You're more likely to associate the extent of his commitment to going natural with putting his feet up and drinking organic green tea. That's why, rather than go into the fields with manure, seeds and shovel to grow cotton the natural way, he decided to design and sell a line of trendy T-shirts.

'The tees are made of organic cotton and printed with non-polluting inks. Organic farming is sustainable because the pesticides don't leach out the nutrients and leave the soil fallow. So farmers can plant year after year. No debt, no pollution, no suicides, no nastiness,' says Apu, whose line is called 'No Nasties'. He's wearing one of his own T-shirts, black with part of the Hindi alphabet lettered on it in white. 'Mine are simple, smart tees with an accent on design.'

Growing up, Bombay boy Apu didn't have grand plans for himself or the world. He just wanted to be happy. So he floated along with the rest of his class, doing the conventional things that were meant to bring contentment—studying engineering in Mumbai, a masters' degree at the University of Texas at Austin in the US in the late 1990s, followed by a series of challenging jobs. He worked in tech management and product design in Travelocity, Epoch Securities, Scient and Frog Design in New York and San Francisco, and for about a year at Deloitte in Sydney, Australia.

'The quality of work was great. I was with teams doing innovative, cutting-edge stuff,' he says. He was paid well, about $150,000 a year, and life was good—comfortable enough for a couple of vacations anywhere in the world every year, and good wine every day. 'No worries,' he says.

This was until sometime in 2007 when he came across an article online that described Maharashtra's cotton-growing region as 'the suicide belt' because 270,000 farmers had killed themselves since 1995 after being bankrupted by BT cotton cultivation, unfair trade practices and high debts. 'The facts and numbers stuck in my head and became a growing pain, a thorn in my side. It was shocking to read that cotton cultivation was just not viable. My life gradually began to feel too far removed from real problems,' he said. 'I wanted to do something, contribute in some way.'

Apu began making plans with his wife Shweta, but it would be four years before he gathered the courage to make the jump. He wanted to do more than just write a cheque for a charity and knew straight out that he did not want to start a non-profit. He started doing some reading and found that there were a lot of government and private initiatives at the grassroots level to get farmers to switch to organic and sustainable agricultural practices by abandoning genetically modified seeds and chemical fertilizers and pesticides. Also gaining ground was the fair-trade movement to ensure that farmers and primary producers get a better deal and are paid enough for their labour by cutting out middlemen and moneylenders.

Farmers were aware of the alternatives but reluctant to switch because there weren't enough people buying organic and fair-trade products. These products are usually priced at a premium because the demand is lower as consumers tend to look for the best price for themselves rather than for the producer as well.

'Teach a man to fish, and you feed him for life. But what if there's no market to sell the fish?' Apu asks. He decided to tackle the lack of a market and create demand for and awareness about organic and fair-trade products in India. The idea behind the fair-trade movement is to get the customer and producer to partner up—everyday shopping can be a statement against inequality by just choosing to buy a product that sends back a fair price to the farmer.

Apu wanted to start his own clothing line to prove that organic, fair trade could be affordable, but he just couldn't commit to the idea. 'I dilly-dallied for more than two years. The decision was finally made by Shweta, as she wanted to return and pursue her own career in design here. Once that life-altering decision was made, it gave me the impetus to change my career and finally take the leap into this business,' he says. It helped that a lot of their Indian friends from the US were also moving back to set up their own businesses or take up jobs here. 'That also gave me the confidence to return home and try to start over.'

Back in Mumbai in February 2010, after taking a year and a half to wind up their lives in the US, Apu began making plans and looking for partners. The idea was to create regular, everyday clothing that was ethically manufactured and sourced, and by October he had settled on T-shirts—he loved well-designed tees, they were easy to make and would connect instantly with young people.

'I don't believe that anyone who is truly aware of what is going on would turn their back on it and continue to support this unsustainable economy,' he says. What was needed to create a market was a viable alternative that didn't ask consumers to change their lifestyle, and matched their fashion and design sensibilities. 'The idea was to let people do what they normally do, wear what they like to wear—just help them make informed decisions and choose well while shopping,' he says.

He met designer and photographer Diti Kotecha while training with the Mumbai Ultimate Frisbee team and they decided to band together. 'I don't have a brain wired for business, I'm more creative. So most of my "planning" related to ideation, branding and design,' says Apu. That meant costing and financial projections were rather back-of-the-envelope with the initial investment of Rs 8 lakh coming out of his savings account. Apu's approach has been and continues to be 'get started and things will happen'.

The laidback style has meant fumbling in the dark, banking on happy accidents and working things out the hard way. It took him a while to figure out the supply chain by getting in touch with farmers' groups and fair-trade organizations.

The first partnership he forged with non-governmental organization Shop for Change, for instance, happened by chance—a friend invited him to a pizza-making class where he saw a Shop for Change jhola bag. He came back home, googled them and realized that the fair-trade labelling organization, which promotes social equality, had all the contacts he needed to get in touch with farmers' collectives growing organic cotton and factories manufacturing T-shirts. 'I didn't need to reinvent the wheel,' he says.

Apu launched No Nasties on 15 April 2011 with most of the business being done online. From Day 1, he decided to go the e-commerce way with www.nonasties.in, though a few stores around the country do stock his tees. 'I felt I could talk to customers directly if I sold online and explained what

I was trying to do. I still interact with each buyer personally, on the phone, Facebook or by email,' he says.

Selling online not only helps small, niche businesses target the customer they're looking for and get instant feedback but also provides the pat on the back they crave. 'I love hearing from people from literally all corners of the world about how happy they are to see our website and read about what we are doing. I love emails from customers after they receive our T-shirts in the post saying that they absolutely love them!'

The cotton cultivation, fabric, dyes and manufacturing process for No Nasties meet the requirements of Global Organic Textile Standards, internationally accepted environmental criteria along the organic textiles supply chain, which also demands compliance with certain globally formulated social criteria. In October 2013, No Nasties got a license from Fairtrade International (FLO), the international organization that has drawn up the principles of fair trade. No Nasties T-shirts now carry a fair-trade tag, which means every constituent of the final product is sourced in a sustainable manner. 'The tag helps in a market where people cut corners and make claims that aren't necessarily true. Customers are quite sceptical and price-conscious so having the licence gives us greater recognition,' he says.

It isn't just for the market to recognize what he's trying to do. For a small company that lurches into trouble now and then, getting past FLO's strict filters to be the first Indian T-shirt company to carry the circular green-and-blue logo is a sort of reward, a kind of appreciation that makes the struggle worth it.

'Every day, I think I'm mad to have done this. I miss my easy life in the US. I miss the salary and the comfort. It's not easy to adjust to India,' says Apu. 'I'm struggling but I know I'll get there and these are the little things that make you say, Yay!'

Less than a year into the launch, Diti moved on. 'That hit me and I lost a few months dealing with that,' he says, asking that the reasons for Diti's departure not be documented. Design drives No Nasties and they suddenly found themselves without a designer. 'We couldn't find a good graphic designer after that so we couldn't launch new designs for a while,' he says. Shweta, who has a background in fashion, began pitching in and she now oversees most of the design.

Apu cast the net wider, started taking in interns and kept the work going. 'They're enthusiastic and we keep getting fresh ideas,' he says. UnLtd India, an incubator for social entrepreneurs, spotted No Nasties and gave it Rs 80,000 for the first year, and Rs 2 lakh for 2012–13. That covered marketing and event costs. 'More than the financial assistance, the business planning, mentoring and networking from UnLtd was invaluable,' he says.

Apu's technology and web experience helped build the online presence, his product development knowledge was channelled towards ideation, and management expertise from past jobs helped oversee the ever-changing team. He was sure that he had a good brand and a great product because demand was higher than supply, but struggles with manufacturing made it hard to build momentum and grow. 'We broke even in our first year, but I didn't take home any real profits, so it is still a challenge.' The plan for the next year is to 'get to financial sustainability and then to profitability.' He isn't afraid of other brands entering the space because he says the real challenge right now is expanding the customer base and getting people to choose organic and fair-trade products. 'Only once that happens will brands want to enter the space. Competition is not a bad thing. It means prices will eventually go down.'

Though No Nasties has turned the corner, Apu still doesn't take home a salary, living instead off savings and returns on investments made when he worked in the corporate world. And he's still searching for happiness. 'That's all I wanted all my life, I'm still looking for it,' he says.

In January 2014, Apu and Shweta moved No Nasties's headquarters from Mumbai to Arpora, a village in north Goa. 'Goa offers more calmness, more mental bandwidth, more time to work, better quality of life. It's cheaper to expand and set up a bigger office and warehouse—all things that are nearly impossible in Mumbai,' he says.

In October that year, he expanded No Nasties from just T-shirts to an entire clothing line. The funky printed tees have made way for dresses, tank tops, polo shirts and V-necked tees as the company's customer base moved from college students to twenty-five- to forty-five-year-old working professionals.

In 2014, No Nasties started working with Armstrong Knitting Mills in Tirupur, one of the leading manufacturers of sustainable clothing in India. Not only is the factory organic and fair-trade certified but it is also carbon neutral, having its own wind turbine and solar energy farms. No Nasties also expanded its cotton sourcing to three suppliers to allow for more flexibility in the supply chain.

'We're now India's first 100 per cent organic, fair-trade clothing brand,' says Apu, who crowdfunded the launch with a 'Give Us a Kick' campaign on Facebook and his website to pre-sell gift cards priced from Rs 1000 to Rs 25,000. Unfortunately, 2014 was a challenging year as No

Nasties changed one of its manufacturers, and tees for both the spring and summer collections didn't pass quality-control checks. Without new designs online, sales stagnated and they were running low on cash.

'We needed financial assistance and thought it would be best to ask our supporters directly,' he says. Instead of asking for donations, he asked people to buy No Nasties gift cards which they could redeem against clothes once the new collection launched. No Nasties raised about Rs 3.5 lakh in two weeks. 'It worked really well.'

Over the next three years, he wants No Nasties not only to grow into a brand people think of first when they hear 'organic fair-trade clothing' but also have the footprint to create more consumer awareness and have more direct involvement with farmers. 'If I could go back, I'd aim for No Nasties to be a lot bigger from the start,' says Apu. 'After four years, we're still a small business. Not sure if I've done justice to the idea yet.'

APU'S ADVICE

1. Starting your own business means forgoing a lot of the comfort you were used to. The trade-off is that you're happier. Keep that in mind.
2. Have a business plan in place and make sure it's aligned to your values. Stay true to yourself.
3. Be prepared to lose a lot of sleep!

TAKING THE PLUNGE

Snehal Bhal

After nine years in banking, Snehal Bhal decided to make a career of her passion for swimming. She is an international masters' class swimmer, plays water polo at the state level, and is one of the few certified aqua-fitness trainers in India.

Snehal Bhal never gets the Monday morning blues. By the time her friends are getting to their offices, she's finished work for the day and is sitting by her window, watching the world rush by.

The thirty-six-year-old aqua-fitness trainer is done with all her classes and is home by 10 a.m., the time she used to start her day in the bank until five years ago. 'I often message my banker friends saying I'm relaxing and eating cereal, just to irritate them because I know it's the start of a stressful day for them,' she says, her pixie-like face breaking into a grin.

Aqua-fitness combines cardio and toning workouts with swimming, and Snehal is quite the relentless trainer, pushing seven of her students to keep going on a nippy January morning at the Bombay Gymkhana, one of the five clubs she teaches at. 'The water is cold,' protests the only man in the class. The members, all in their mid-fifties, are a cheery lot, aiming to slowly but steadily lose weight and build strength and flexibility, which aqua-fitness is known for. 'So let's go faster to keep you warm,' Snehal calls, throwing in some bendy sticks of fluorescent foam to work with. As the aqua noodles hit the water and float, the members paddle across and grab them, the only props they'll be using during the hour-long workout. Despite the pace and the tough workout, there's time for corny puns and laughter, good-natured splashing and mock fights.

Snehal learnt to swim as a child but took to it seriously about seven years ago, because the long hours behind a desk had left her feeling weak and unhealthy. She started with a couple of laps a day and graduated to ten laps as her stamina grew. 'Slowly, I went up to swimming forty laps a day, seven days a week,' she says. A colleague at the bank toted up the numbers and told her she was swimming close to a kilometre a day. 'I realized I was addicted,' she says.

She found herself a coach and began training in earnest with the idea of competing in the masters' class, a category for older swimmers. Finding a coach was the first challenge since most only want to train younger people who show promise of becoming professionals. 'Swimming was just a serious hobby. I was doing well at the bank,' she says. After finishing her masters in management studies at Mumbai University, Snehal had joined ICICI Lombard as a product manager and later moved to HSBC as a marketing manager for wealth management services. 'I had lots of exciting projects and the teams I worked with were great,' says Snehal, who was born in Nagpur in 1978 and moved to Mumbai after class ten. In March 2009, a routine medical test showed up a cyst in her breast, which doctors suspected was cancerous and operated on to remove. The first question she asked the doctor when she woke up in the recovery room after surgery was: When can I swim again?

Tests showed it was a benign cyst but the week in hospital gave Snehal time to think. 'That kind of uncertainty makes you reflect on what you really want from life,' she says.

During the two weeks of recovery, she missed the feel of the water and the scent of chlorine, but not the office and its environment. 'It made me think about career and passion. I enjoyed work, I was doing well, I liked my team, but why didn't I miss it? I spent most of my day at the bank and just a couple of hours in the pool. But I missed swimming, not work. Something was wrong. I wanted a job that made me happy, a job that I truly loved, the way I loved to swim,' she says.

It was the first time she considered a career related to swimming. The obvious choice was to become a coach. 'There is a demand for women coaches but they don't get paid very well, and that was not what I wanted to do. It didn't seem exciting enough,' she says. Further, the work would be seasonal. Swimming classes fill up in the summer and taper off once the holidays end; students too tend to drop out of regular classes once they pick up the basics. She started exploring options that would keep her in chlorine yet out of penury. 'I was used to the independence of earning my own money and the security of a steady job,' says Snehal. Her coach suggested aqua-fitness, a cardio and muscle-toning fitness routine done in the swimming pool, which is popular abroad but little known in India. It seemed perfect—fitness training in a swimming pool. It was exactly the kind of thing she had been looking for when she started swimming. 'I did my research and decided to give it a shot. I discussed it with my family and they were just as enthusiastic. They understood my need to find work that I enjoyed.'

In September 2009, Snehal took some time off work and joined Federation of International Sports, Aerobics and Fitness in Singapore to do a certification course in aqua-fitness. Many international-level sports teams use aqua-fitness for cross-training because it's known to strengthen muscles. 'I enjoyed it. In the corporate world, I'd always been part of a team, but here I was learning to lead. Everything about the course was new and exciting yet it felt familiar since I loved the water,' she says. 'But I still didn't believe this could be a full-time career. I didn't have the guts to leave a safe and secure job.' Back in Mumbai at the end of November, Snehal went to a few clubs near her home to ask if they'd be willing to take her on. 'At first I had to explain what aqua-fitness was. No one was aware of it,' she says. The club in Goregaon, where she had been swimming regularly, offered her a weekend slot. She was also swimming competitively as well as playing for the Mumbai women's water polo team while working at the bank.

The club put up a poster, and the first few students came rather hesitantly to try out something that seemed unusual. 'I explained that it was a good way to lose weight while building stamina,' she says. Regular swimming follows a rhythm—you breathe and move with a rhythm, so once your body gets used to the routine, you can do up to forty laps a day without really losing weight though you build stamina. Snehal's aqua-fitness routines are designed to vary the movements in the water so that you get a complete body workout while gaining strength and stamina, and losing weight.

'I let people do a free trial class when I first started teaching at the Goregaon club,' she says. Within a couple of months she had ten students. 'I kept thinking people would drop out but they didn't. You know how it is with fitness classes, people are enthusiastic at first but then get busy or just bored.' This didn't seem to happen with her classes. 'They found it addictive, like I had. More people wanted to join, and the club wanted extra batches,' she says.

The chance to have some fun while getting into shape is irresistible. 'It doesn't seem like a workout,' says one of her students after the class. 'Soon, you realize that you feel more energetic and have lost a few inches,' she says.

By August 2010, Snehal was convinced she could make a career out of it. 'Until then, it had been a vague dream,' she says. 'I wanted to make a name for myself as a swimmer, not as a banker.' It wasn't easy to decide to be financially dependent on her husband since she had always earned enough to support herself. 'My biggest fear was the money, but my husband encouraged me to choose what made me happy. He said, "If you don't try, you will never know if it can work." Plus, I seriously believed I would, some day, earn more than I did at the bank.'

She made a deal with herself: She would earn enough from aqua-fitness to cover her needs within a year or go back to the corporate world. Snehal's biggest expense is swimming gear—caps, suits, waterproof watches, goggles and the rest. 'I had to be realistic about the fact that I would not be getting a fixed salary every month, but aqua-fitness was what made me happy and I had to make the trade-off.'

Her father, a senior government officer for whom job security is paramount, had his apprehensions. He worried that the income would not be steady since people would not come to class during vacations, children's exams, the monsoon, winter, when they got bored, when they felt lazy . . . 'I had to make a presentation to him on how I planned to increase my earnings year-on-year. He made me work out how many clubs I would have to work at to earn Rs X. It was good to have a harsh critic. It made me plan for the lean months. He still jokes that this is not a sustainable career, and wants me to return to the corporate world,' she says.

When she resigned in August 2010, the bank offered her a sabbatical. 'I had been promoted to associate vice president in March that year. I considered it but I knew I'd never give aqua-fitness a serious shot till I was pushed into a corner and had to make a living from it,' she says.

Once she quit, Snehal began doing the rounds of clubs in Mumbai and realized that most people had no idea what she was talking about. 'Even if I convinced a club to give me a slot, getting students to enrol was my responsibility,' she says. It was a bit of a disappointment since classes had gone so well at the club in Goregaon. 'You have to work hard to get students into the water. It's not like a regular business where you can offer a service and people walk in for it,' she says.

Her early breaks came through friends, students and other coaches who had seen her work and told potential students and other clubs about her. In many ways, her students have been her biggest advertisers. 'One person loves it, tells his or her friends about it. Those friends ask their clubs to let me do a trial class . . . and so it goes,' she says. 'It takes a lot of time but I've found that if a person comes once, he or she is usually hooked,' she says.

At the Bombay Gymkhana, the members hold and move the aqua noodles different ways while paddling across the length of the pool. The body is lighter when it's in water, making physical effort less of a strain, and the natural resistance of the water increases the impact of the workout. Those who aren't strong swimmers stay in the shallow end and cover the breadth of the pool. 'Even people who don't know how to swim can do aqua-fitness because most of the routines are done in the shallow end, and the water's buoyancy helps you,' she says. As if to illustrate the point, a woman who was complaining of a shoulder strain caused by bad sleeping posture at the beginning of class calls out from the water that she's able to stretch her arm farther without too much pain. 'The water reduces the risk of injury and strengthens weak joints,' says Snehal.

She has altered routines to include techniques she's learnt as a water-polo player and a swimmer to keep classes engaging and monotony at bay. 'My routine is a combination of aerobics, cardio, muscle toning and fun so that people enjoy it,' she says. Competition is still low in her field, with just a couple of others doing what she does. 'There are enough clubs and pools in Mumbai, plus I got an early start and keep varying my routine,' she says.

Snehal has kept the deal she made with herself and now earns more than she did in the corporate world, and has started building up her savings again. 'My vision is to have an institute where I can train people in aqua-fitness. I haven't even started planning that but I know it will happen. Aqua-fitness and swimming are my passion,' she says. 'I no longer have days when I want to skip work because I just don't feel like going.'

SNEHAL'S TIPS TO DO WHAT YOU LOVE

1. Take the plunge. You can't hold a job *and* chase your dream. Until you are pushed into a corner, you are not going to get out there and find a way to make your idea work.
2. Be regular and disciplined in whatever you do. As a fitness instructor, you can't take vacations or a day off just like that. Clients make time to come to your class and enjoy it, so you have to be committed.
3. Be enthusiastic. Unless you are 100 per cent enthusiastic all the time, you can't motivate others to stay fit or lose weight.

LEARNING TO TEACH

Vikram Bhat

Vice president of an equities firm on Wall Street to vice principal of a school in Bangalore, that's the switch Vikram Bhat made because he wanted to see every child have a shot at entering college.

A section of the street has been blocked off with school benches and a marching band has taken up formation and is enthusiastically turning the national anthem into a series of clangs, bangs and thuds. On the balconies and terraces of the houses on the street, men in white vests and women drying their hair are waiting to watch the local school hoist the flag for Independence Day. Children stand in the middle of the street in uniforms of varying shades of white, holding cardboard cones that sprout strips of saffron, white and green paper, ready to wave the craft-class-made bouquets to the beat of the drum. The non-performing students squeeze into wriggling lines, craning their necks to catch a glimpse of the show.

Confused by the unseemly activity on its street, a dog makes a dash for the relative safety of the empty school premises. Sticks and shouts come out and a couple of boys chase the frightened creature. The vice principal appears and talks to the dog for a few minutes to calm it down. He walks a few paces and the dog starts following. Once they reach the bench-boundary, the dog hops on to it and looks up at him. After a few minutes, it tires of sitting and staring, jumps off and runs away. 'Now you can train dogs too, sir,' calls out a wit among the group of boys that has been watching Vikram Bhat, vice principal of My School, a school in a low-income neighbourhood in Bangalore, firmly but gently lead the dog away.

Street-side shows of patriotism or of persuasion weren't always Vikram's scene. In 2008, when he was vice president of Portfolio Trading at Sanford C. Bernstein, a premier investment research and brokerage firm on Wall Street in the heart of the financial district in New York, a vague sense of dissatisfaction made him re-examine the path his life was taking. After trying his hand at a clutch of careers, he decided that education was his calling and returned to India to retrain as a teacher.

'My primary reason for doing what I'm doing today is this idea of waking up every day and feeling a strong purpose about what I do,' says Vikram, a snub-nosed thirty-nine-year-old with a wide, boyish grin. 'I didn't want to head to work every morning as a matter of routine.'

Growing up in Mumbai in the 1980s, Vikram loved sports, and played state-level tennis and football and cricket for his school, but faced the dilemma that most students do after class nine—studies or sports. 'Of course I didn't have the confidence to make a career out of sports so I chose to focus on academics,' he says. School done, he went to engineering college and found a job with a tech firm at the end of four years.

The idea that he had not enjoyed college and engineering because of the atmosphere nagged at him, so he resigned after a couple of years and left Mumbai in 1999 to do a postgraduate degree in computer science at New York University, hoping to discover a love for his chosen profession. 'I didn't particularly enjoy that either but my tuition fees left me in the hole. So I took a job writing code in an IT firm to pay off my debt,' he says.

After switching a couple of jobs, he ended up at a firm that developed software for traders. 'While writing code to automate trading systems, I started to figure out how traders think and realized, "I could do this job. It would bring in four times the money",' he says. When a position opened up for a technology guy at Sanford C Bernstein in 2004, he jumped jobs and soon moved to the trading desk.

'I loved trading. There's an alpha-male part of you that thrives on the energy and the aggression. You're working with really clever people with a wide range of interests, you're learning every day, and the money is great,' he says, while connecting his laptop to his TV to show a video of a university marching band's tribute to Michael Jackson. Vikram and his wife Rajani have endless curiosity for all things, and days spent with them can include everything from watching movies, planning holidays and picking your way through a handicraft fair to getting your first taste of molecular gastronomy and a crash course in Arsenal's history.

While he was a techie, Vikram created solutions that helped the trading desk estimate the impact of its orders as well as analyse stock movements after trade, essentially building software to enhance the efficiency of trading. Once he made the shift to the trading desk, since his background was in IT, he did research and analysis and created products for the buying and selling of stocks using technology. 'I've made two big switches in my career—technology to trading, then trading to teaching,' says Vikram.

Since the work at Sanford C. Bernstein involved forecasting and analysis, it demanded detailed research into the way industries work and a thorough understanding of different sectors. 'Your area may be technology but you develop an interest in a range of subjects from economics to history because you need to look at a development from five or six angles before taking a position,' he says. 'You meet people with different world views. It's a very stimulating environment and there's a lot of humour on the desk. Sometimes, I still miss that.'

In 2005, he and Rajani, a pulmonologist in training, enrolled in a weekly Vedanta philosophy class that a friend told them about. They started the classes with mere curiosity but found them thought-provoking. Questions that are often shelved came to the fore—why am I here, am I living a life with purpose, do I make a difference? Their teacher didn't speak of happiness but of contentment and of not wanting more, which ran diametrically opposite to the greed-is-good philosophy of Wall Street.

'The classes were a catalyst. It no longer seemed enough to work for a fixed fifty hours a week and earn a lot of money,' says Vikram. In hindsight, the answers and explanations come easily to him but at that moment it was all quite confusing because he enjoyed his work and was good at it yet it didn't bring contentment.

Across the dining table was Rajani—as a resident doctor on a fellowship in the US, she earned about a tenth of what he did, worked far longer hours, and dealt with more stress yet she was happier. 'You just feel that money doesn't buy that much,' he says. They talked about his sense of fatigue, uncharacteristic for someone as driven, energetic and upbeat as him. 'I seemed to check most of the midlife crisis boxes—at thirty-one,' he says, laughing.

Rather than reconcile himself to it, he set to work to understand what was causing the haze of world-weariness. 'My work life seemed pointless. Working on Wall Street is something you dream of doing but it doesn't make a difference. You just make the rich richer, and that gnaws at you. I'm very critical of the system now that I'm out of it,' he says. 'What is the point of what I do? That is a question that keeps coming back at you.'

It took him a while to admit to himself that his work gave him joy but was not soul-satisfying. 'Rajani and I discussed it for nearly a year, and she understood why I had to make a change and encouraged it. I didn't know what I was going to do, but I knew I had to stop doing what I was doing for everything to become clearer.'

Vikram is the quintessential operations guy. He plans, organizes and prepares for everything—he has a spreadsheet with his month's wardrobe listed to cut time spent on unnecessary decision-making every morning. So the first step after resolving to quit was looking into his savings.

'I'm pretty boring that way. My thought process is quite structured and my decisions are not spontaneous,' he says. Rajani's fellowship would end in 2009, and both wanted to return to India. 'By the end of 2006, I knew I wanted a change in my life. So most of 2007 was spent planning our savings to understand how much we would need to live a decent life and what changes we would have to make to give up the salary I was earning,' he says. They paid off all their debts, bought another apartment in Bangalore, where their parents lived, to ensure a steady income from rent, and started scaling down. He quit in March 2008 after the bonus for the previous year was paid.

Within a week of his last day, Vikram was planning his search for his new life. 'The moment I was done with my trading job and didn't have a set routine, I was a little unsettled and worried. So I quickly settled into what I do best—planning,' he says. He made a long list of the things he'd always been interested in, the things he'd imagined himself doing and the things he'd like to do. 'I spent a year exploring everything on that list,' he says. 'When you have this romantic idea of a career, you must break it down to what it looks like on a day-to-day basis and see if it still excites you. From 20,000 ft away, everything looks great.'

Sports management, education and films were high on that list. He did a short course on screenplay-writing in New York, organized a couple of film festivals for the local Indian community and made a short film with a friend. 'It was fun but not really what I wanted to do. It was a process of elimination to find out what I wanted to do,' he says.

He moved on to the next item on his list—sports management. Vikram felt young Indians could do with the kind of professional management and mentoring that go into promising sportspeople's careers in the US. 'You've seen *Moneyball*?,' he asks, referring to the 2011 film starring Brad Pitt that was nominated for six Oscars. 'That kind of work, you scout for talent, nurture it.' From his own experience as a state-level tennis player who abandoned the sport, he knew that the right mentor would have been able to nudge him to the next level. He met sports management teams in the US and one in India and was drawn to the idea of pushing young athletes harder, but there was one more very big item to cross off his list before beginning his professional life again—education.

Indian schooling had always been a hot topic of conversation at NRI parties and dinners, and Vikram was intrigued by the idea of equity in education. At that time, he wasn't really keen on being a teacher but felt there were ways in which he could make schools in India more efficient and effective.

Since Vikram believes serious changemakers need to work with and fix existing systems rather than reinvent the wheel by starting their own organizations, he began looking for institutions he could fit into both in India and the US.

One organization whose goal appealed to him was Uncommon Schools, which runs programmes in the New York area to ensure that students from low-income groups and the African American community have a shot at getting into college and challenge the idea that they can't do well in school. 'Their mission—every child should get a bachelor's degree—resonated with me. They believe that children from underprivileged families should get the same opportunities as those from wealthier ones. I wanted to do something like that in India. Of course, the problem is far more basic here—250 million school-going children and only one in 10 will finish school; can you imagine where we will be in fifty years? It's going to be like the French Revolution. It's not going to end well.'

For four months from March to June 2009, he interned with Uncommon Schools, learning about classroom techniques, creating a strong school culture and separating operations from instruction, and worked with its founder Doug Lemov, considered one of the foremost thinkers on education in the US. Lemov believes that great teaching is largely about consistent behaviour, which can be taught to and learnt by aspiring teachers, and this consistent behaviour eventually evolves into the school's culture. 'A lot of his ideas are universal techniques and I wanted to adapt them to India,' says Vikram.

The idea that excited him the most was separating operations from instruction, which involves appointing a person to take care of the minutiae like day-to-day administration, filing reports and keeping track of attendance and budgets, so that the principal is free to focus on academic achievement. 'Incredible efficiency comes in when you do this. People like me who enjoy ops are great to track procurement and budgets. Principals rarely enjoy that kind of work, so if you take it away, not only do academic results improve but they enjoy their jobs too. I was sure it was not being done in India and wanted to try it,' says Vikram. 'I wanted to bring that kind of professionalism into education.'

In 2009, Vikram and Rajani moved from New York to Bangalore and restarted life. 'We both struggled with the work culture and with settling back in. We had lived in the US for ten years, it's hard not to miss it,' says Rajani. 'You have to be very clear about what India offers otherwise you will not be able to make it. For us, the closeness to family and friends was important and so we made the shift.'

In August, Vikram started work at Parikrma Humanity Foundation in Bangalore at a fraction of the salary he'd been making before. Parikrma, founded by Shukla Bose, is a non-profit organization that runs four schools for children from slums with the mission to provide them an excellent education and put them on an equal footing with their counterparts from richer families. 'I liked their ideas and they seemed open to the ones I had,' he says.

For a year, he looked after operations and tried introducing systems he'd learnt in the US, but felt he needed to be closer to the classroom. 'To be truly productive in a school environment, I realized one has to be involved with the children and interact with them on a regular basis,' he says. From year two, he began teaching middle-school English and science at the Jayanagar school. 'The first day in the classroom was a real eye-opener. I knew that my class was a challenging one behaviourally, but the extent of noise overwhelmed me,' he says.

Vikram started by making the children draw their dreams on paper and introduced to the class values of love, trust and respect. 'My mentor, Sabitha Raghunath, who was the principal then, supported me in planning and execution for science but I felt a bit unsure about teaching English. I started with a prose lesson 'Packing for a Picnic' and felt quite good about it. I talked about my life, why I had decided to start teaching, about the places I had visited and the people who were important to me.'

Vikram is charming and quick-to-smile, showing a great deal of love and warmth while dealing with every single person who crosses his path, from security guard to next-floor neighbour with whom most people just have a nodding acquaintance. While teaching a class, there's a perceptible change—the easy assurance makes for a relaxed yet brisk classroom manner; the characteristic smile and warmth is in place but there's an edge of authority and a firm hand to show who the boss is.

This is the classroom behaviour that Vikram's mentor Sabitha later described as 'walking the thin line of love and discipline'. Vikram gives a great deal of himself and expresses his fondness for the students through his attitude and gestures yet commands and demands respect as their teacher and guide. One of his students from Parikrma, Nandini, later explains how Vikram-anna sparked her interest in English and poetry by reading Wordsworth and Walt Whitman to the class 'with feeling plus full meaning'. After class, he would play football with them, read to them or, most memorably, help them put together a morning assembly inspired by the British theatrical percussion group Stomp, after they told him they wanted to create their own music.

Most people who meet Vikram are carried away by the nobility of what he's done but it's soon apparent that his sense of purpose is tempered by realism and a sense of humour, which keeps him clear of being a sanctimonious goody-goody. He's always enjoyed cracking complex problems, and the classroom is the kind of place that presents a new one every day. 'I love what I do and I enjoy it but people often forget that teachers are also like everyone else. There's no missionary zeal. Teaching is hard work, and unless your teachers are paid competitively, you're never going to attract and retain good talent,' he says.

When Vikram started teaching at Parikrma, he found himself blindsided not just by the amount of energy it drew but also by the variance in the abilities of the children in the class—some class-six students were reading at the level of second-graders. After ten years at a fairly sedentary job, Vikram was unprepared for the demands of being on his feet all day. He lost six kilos in the first two months. 'You just don't expect that kind of physical stress. Managing classrooms takes a lot out of new teachers.' Another unexpected challenge was being confronted with value-based questions: Why shouldn't I beat others, what's wrong about stealing? 'I worried a lot about whether I would be able to connect with the kids, if they would listen to me and if I would be able to teach them anything. I still worry about that last one,' he says.

The shift was a slow one filled with moments of doubt, frustration, despair and absolute joy. 'I came with very high expectations. When you make a move like this you come with a lot of impatience about how quickly you're going to find satisfaction, and how you're going to fuel the kind of dramatic transformation you see in films. It doesn't work that way,' he says.

His mentor Sabitha urged him to understand the personality and motivations of each child. 'In teaching, the rewards come so slowly,' says Vikram. 'It played on my mind that I had sacrificed so much money for something that didn't seem very fulfiling, but I just had to focus on the larger goal.'

A shift like Vikram's is fuelled entirely by belief in a larger purpose. For him, it was his belief that in urban poor communities, a high level of literacy is particularly important as it opens up varied life possibilities, and a desire to do his bit to act on his convictions. 'It's not like I'm always upbeat. There are low points but you just find ways around it.' Often, he felt that though the organizations he was working with did good work, their ideas and ways of working didn't match his. When disillusionment set in, Vikram drew on ideas picked up from the Vedanta philosophy classes—if you commit to a course of action that is unselfish, the gains are lasting.

Long-distance running, which he had started in New York, helped clear his mind and bring his focus back to his goals, and he started training for marathons. The solitary hours on the road to build physical endurance also stoked his staying power. 'I revisited the reason why I had made the decision to leave Wall Street and move to India. I realized that the shift was not just to make myself feel good about teaching poor children, but also to raise standards of education and opportunities for all children. Once you commit to a goal that is larger than yourself, there is joy,' he says.

After three years at Parikrma, Vikram moved to Teach for India, a non-profit that enlists young graduates and professionals to teach for two years in low-income schools. Its mission, 'In fifty years, all children will attain an excellent education', resonated with him. As its expansion and recruitment manager, he went back to an all-operations role, optimising processes, looking at the number of low-income, English-speaking public schools, the different laws in each city, and deciding where to place fellows. The idea was to gain countrywide perspective of the challenges in education.

One of the things he struggled with was coming to terms with the fact that most NGOs don't place a premium on deadlines. Coming from the corporate world where deadlines and professionalism are the norm, the easy-going pace of the NGO world was hard to accept. 'Companies are competitive, they're constantly trying to solve problems and be more efficient. We need that kind of impatience in the education sector too if we really want better results,' he says.

Again, it was time to think about what he wanted to do and reorient his goals. After two jobs in the NGO sector, he had reservations about working for another non-profit but was convinced that education was his calling. The pull of the classroom was a constant and in June 2013, he enrolled at Bangalore's Christ College to get his BEd so that he would be professionally qualified to teach full-time in the government or the private sector.

Vikram found himself the oldest in the class but among the most enthusiastic for a curriculum that was well structured, and the professors stoked his desire to learn. He finished as class valedictorian in March 2014 and joined My School the next month as its vice principal.

Since he's been there, says Principal Vidya B.S., whose father founded the school, the children and teachers have pulled up their socks and there's new energy. Some of the activities Vikram has introduced include physical education, kalari, dance, art classes and special-themed assemblies done by different classes. 'Children really connect with him and follow his lead. His enthusiasm is infectious,' she says.

Vikram's approach is to lead by example and focus on small actions that contribute to overall change. Since he joined My School in June 2014, for instance, he has been getting to work before 8 a.m. every day. At 8.10 a.m., he is at the gate greeting each student and teacher who walks in with a smile or a word or two. As the second bell sounds at 8.15 a.m., students rush towards the gate and Vikram's smile has disappeared. He doesn't acknowledge any greetings; parents who are dropping children off look rather shamefaced, knowing they've been spotted bringing children in late. The students get two more minutes to squeeze in before the gates are closed. Latecomers line up and a monitor goes down the queue adding names to a list. They'll have to do detention after school, an hour of extra time for being late. Punctuality has risen from about 70 per cent to 90 per cent after Vikram started gate duty. Teachers too are rarely late now. 'Earlier, students who were late had to miss the first hour of class or go home, which didn't really serve as a punishment. Being made to stay back after school has more of an impact. Teaching is really about setting examples and holding children to really high expectations. So if they see that I'm there early, they start making the effort to be on time,' he says.

On Independence Day, Vidya has a surprise for him before the flag is hoisted. They go upstairs to the library—a door as grey as all the others along the narrow corridor opens up to reveal the kind of room that helps transport you to a fantasy land, which is what reading can do. A blue whale, a surgeonfish, an octopus and other brightly coloured creatures of the deep are suspended from the ceiling. The large creatures were created and painted for a special assembly Vikram helped the children put together a few months before, and teachers have spent a large part of the previous evening suspending them from the library ceiling. 'Earlier, we might have just thrown them out or stored them in an attic. Instead, we came up with an idea to use them and brighten up the school,' says Vidya.

Changing the culture of a school—from the usual one of hierarchy and fear to an open, energetic yet disciplined one—is a tough task but one Vikram believes is crucial to the goal of achieving educational equity. 'A strong culture is probably the most important and desirable characteristic of an effective school,' he says. 'Once you set the culture, everything else will follow—academic results, motivated teachers, self-confident children who are achievers, everything.'

Many of Vikram's ideas are inspired by his learning from Doug Lemov and Uncommon Schools, and he keeps repeating that it is important to hold students to unwaveringly high expectations. It is this that children respond to best, and his words bear this out during the course of the Independence Day function at My School. Once the festivities move indoors, it's chaos—children refuse to settle down into the rectangular hall that serves as the auditorium, there's noise, shrieks and chattering. A teacher ineffectively talks over them for fifteen minutes until Vikram steps up to the stage. A rustle of sssshhhs goes through the crowd and the decibel level instantly drops to the low buzz that is a constant in any school at any time. 'We will not start until there is silence,' he says. Within minutes, the invocation song begins and though they fidget and squirm their way through the show, the students stay in their seats. Students seem to understand instinctively that he's approachable yet exacting. After the show, students stop by to chat and laugh with him, and he goes across to have a word with almost every one of the pint-sized freedom fighters who paraded across the stage.

To look angry and not be angry is something he's worked hard to succeed at, explains Sabitha. 'Children are quick to understand and reflect what you are thinking and doing,' she says. 'A positive attitude affects them powerfully. They understand that he gives them a lot and therefore expects a lot from them.'

It's a bit like being a doctor, is Rajani's description. 'You cannot switch off; there's no point in your day when you can sit at your desk and pretend to work because you're bored. You have to give 100 per cent all the time, and if you don't, the children realize it,' she says, while we're driving back to their house after the Independence Day celebrations.

Though administrative work takes up a large part of his day, Vikram still teaches social science to class nine students. 'I am nowhere near where I want to be as a teacher. I want students to have better outcomes, better results, and then I will be an effective teacher.'

Over the two years that we've met, Vikram's ideas have shifted though his commitment to bringing professionalism to education hasn't. He's now focused entirely on My School, hoping to create tangible results and influence the lives of the children there so that they go out with a strong sense of who they are and are able to contribute positively to society. 'I have moved away from the idea that I have to change the whole of India. Yes, I had that naïve idea,' he says laughing sheepishly, 'but it's gone in a good way.'

VIKRAM'S LESSON PLAN

1. Build some kind of safety net before you take the plunge. This could mean different things for different people but it's important to have an understanding of your individual financial needs before committing to a life of significantly lower salaries.

2. Get a good sense and a deep understanding of the new career you want to switch to. Read, volunteer, observe and speak to people in that field. Every career seems exciting from the outside, so find out what it's like day-to-day, on the ground. If it still seems appealing, go ahead. With teaching especially, most people tend to romanticize the job, and underestimate how much grit and determination it requires.

3. Once you find your dream job, be prepared to be disappointed. You will have bad days. When you make a move like this, you expect it be awesome from Day One. It won't be because you will still have to deal with people who have the same egos and issues, plus you are starting from zero. So you need a clear goal and infinite patience.

EYE ON THE BALL

Abhijeet Barse

Abhijeet Barse runs Slum Soccer, an organization working to bring about social change through football. In another life, he was a zoology professor and an aquaculture researcher, studying the effects of chemicals in sewage on marine life.

Large cement pipes lying in a field don't sound like the best seats in a stadium. But sheer enthusiasm for a football game between two home teams on a field that's just open space, near a construction site with green-and-blue cones marking the corners and goal posts, makes those cement pipes under a greying monsoon sky seem like Rio de Janeiro's Maracana stadium.

The fans—about ten children—are perched comfortably on the pipes, and watch the boys and girls from their neighbourhood of Godhani in Nagpur warm up by running zigzag around more cones.

The footballers are part of Slum Soccer, a programme run by Krida Vikas Sanstha (KVS), which has been sending underprivileged players from across the country to the Homeless World Cup (a global non-profit encouraging social change through football) every year since 2007. The lessons they learn on the field and from the coaches aren't just about teamwork and scoring goals but also about discipline, self-confidence, health, hygiene, education, fair play, inclusion and more.

Slum Soccer runs close to forty centres across the country—in Maharashtra, Tamil Nadu, Gujarat, Uttarakhand, Madhya Pradesh and West Bengal—promoting development for children through football.

Abhijeet Barse, CEO of Slum Soccer, watches from a distance, leaning against his battered blue, open-top Gypsy that proclaims 'Tottenham Hotspur' on one door and 'Street Football World' on the other. The coach, nineteen-year-old Amol, shouts out directions, and jumps in to demonstrate when someone puts a foot wrong. Abhijeet nods approvingly, and explains, 'The coaches are from the same community the children are from and lead by example whether they're teaching the kids football or using the game for lessons in gender equality.'

Abhijeet's trained to scrutinize, observe, examine and make notes, but his subjects weren't always slum children playing football. He trained as an aquaculture researcher, studying the effect of chemicals in sewage on marine life, and was a researcher in the US and in India before deciding that he needed to do something that had a direct impact on people's lives rather than spend his days in a lab studying fish. 'I guess this is my goldfish bowl now,' he says, laughing.

Abhijeet's an unusual do-gooder—there's no sense of self-righteousness, no sermonizing; he's driven by a desire to reach targets and goals. Dressed in blue jeans, a short-sleeved shirt and grey Adidas trainers with popsicle-orange laces, with a black satchel slung across his shoulder, he looks more like he's waiting for a suburban train rather than someone who's trying to use football as a means to draw street children into a better life.

In a sense, he's inherited KVS from his father, retired physical education lecturer Vijay Barse, who has been helping others for years and had registered the non-governmental organization in 2001. But thirty-seven-year-old Abhijeet has taken a rather circuitous route to arrive on this field.

'Growing up, my father was always doing things for other people—football tournaments, blood donation camps, awareness drives, giving away sports equipment. I didn't think much of it though I knew he was different from other dads. He spent his own money on it, and it all seemed rather ad hoc to me,' says Abhijeet.

Instead, he focused on his studies and his desire to be a scientist. 'The systematic approach of science appealed to me,' he says. Abhijeet finished school in Nagpur, where he was born in 1976, and did his graduation from Ratnagiri's College of Fisheries. After a masters' degree in fisheries science in Mumbai, he did his PhD with a specialization in inland aquaculture at the Central Institute of Fisheries Education.

Abhijeet's research uncovered some disturbing findings—the concentration of chemicals in sewage that was being released into waterways was causing endocrine destruction in fish. Their hormonal patterns were changing and male fish were beginning to behave like the female. 'And that fish goes here,' he says, indicating his stomach. 'Ultimately, we would be the ones affected by our own waste. At that time, I was among the few doing research on the topic in India.'

He published his findings in six international journals and, in 2005, was invited to present a paper at a conference organized by the independent forum Society of Environmental Toxicology and Chemistry in Baltimore in the US. His presentation landed him a job as a researcher with chemical-manufacturing company Rohm and Haas in Philadelphia. 'I knew I was on the right path. My aim had always been to do research and live in the US. I wanted to join a US university as a postdoctoral research fellow,' he says.

Meanwhile, his father was busy—barefoot or *zopadpatti* (slum) football matches every year in slums across the district, a cycle rally for peace to the India-Pakistan border, mini Olympics in 2002, while continuing the blood donation camps. 'When I lived in India, I was not really interested in what he was doing,' says Abhijeet. 'Maybe we really started talking and listening to each other only after I left.'

After a year in the US, Abhijeet was applying for a new job and had to fill in a section called 'Impact Factor'. The impact factor assigned to a publication indicates the average number of times it has been cited in a particular period, and it is often used to measure the importance of the research project. His was five, which is good since the average is between two and three.

Until that moment, he hadn't questioned himself. He'd been happy. Once the doubt crept in, it began to build up. 'It bothered me that the impact of my work would be limited, that I would probably never see the people it would help, that it would be years before governments took my research seriously and banned the release of harmful chemicals.

While my work earned me a name in my field, it would make only me happy. I was becoming limited to just me,' he says, as we bump our way over the rutted roads in his Gypsy towards his office in Bokhara, near Nagpur.

Abhijeet's able to encapsulate his thoughts of that time into about a minute now, but back in 2006, he was wracked with confusion and felt futility in what he was doing. Eleven years of hard work had gone into his higher education, and it all seemed to have very little purpose. Going forward held little appeal, but throwing it all away and starting again was inconceivable.

He tried to convince himself that his research had a higher purpose, that he wasn't the kurta-clad, NGO-type. Conversations with his father left him even more unsettled. Here was a man who gave away much of what he earned and was happy. Abhijeet was on the threshold of everything he'd dreamt of, yet unhappy. He couldn't really get his head around it. He decided to return to India for a while to see if his unhappiness was just a fleeting thing, prompted by homesickness and loneliness, or whether there was a more fulfiling life outside the lab.

He returned to Nagpur at the end of 2006, took up a job in Hislop College and began observing his father's work and 'impact factor'. 'My mother was not happy at all. She knew the difficulties and the money troubles that lay ahead. My father was all for me joining him,' says Abhijeet.

Vijay had started zopadpatti football tournaments in slums in Nagpur and the surrounding districts after he'd seen a bunch of children playing barefoot in the rain with a bucket. The physical education teacher had watched them from beneath a tree as they gleefully splashed through the puddles and scored 'goals' with the battered bucket. He wondered if they'd have more fun with a ball and had returned the next week with a football. And that's how KVS started—by distributing footballs to children in underprivileged communities. Vijay later registered it as an NGO and funded weekend kick-abouts, small tournaments and other events, using his salary.

Abhijeet worked as an assistant professor for three years, while observing KVS on the side, slowly understanding what was right and wrong with his father's approach. 'He had no systems in place, did whatever came to mind, and was always short of funds. I wanted to kick off the programme with an international face, take a more methodical approach,' he says. 'Despite the setbacks I saw his success. I saw how many people's lives had changed. I wanted to reach more people.' Back then, KVS had no count of how many children they were training in the handful of makeshift centres in and around Nagpur. Slum Soccer today has more than 8000 children enrolled in its forty centres across the country. The aim is to reach double the number of children in 2015.

Abhijeet's office is a half-constructed pink building, iron rods still protruding into the sky. The monsoon rain has turned the grass growing wild in front and the trees that surround the building in Bokhara, a semi-rural suburb of Nagpur, a luxuriant shade of green. To the right, a red-and-yellow iron fence encloses a football pitch. It's 10 a.m. on a Monday morning, but seven boys are enthusiastically playing football. 'Today's a school holiday, Nag Panchami,' says Abhijeet as a raucous loudspeaker starts blaring devotional music. 'So they've come early. Otherwise, one or two boys are always playing from the time school finishes.' About 2000 people live in Bokhara, and 100 children come to play at the centre. An hour later only one boy is left but he's still practising. After another hour, a noisy game is on again with more than fifteen boys on the pitch.

A spiral staircase leads to the top floor, which houses Abhijeet's office and the youth centre. Construction of the two-storeyed building proceeded in fits and starts from 2010. It was finally completed in 2014. 'We had to keep stopping work because we would run out of money,' he says. Slum Soccer needs more than Rs 50 lakh a year just to keep all its training centres running—about Rs 1.5 lakh per centre—and the costs go up by about 20 per cent every year.

The walls of his office are painted orange and the shelves hold the trophies that the Slum Soccer teams have won in India and abroad. There's a table in one corner where Abhijeet sets up his laptop, a black-and-white sofa in another, and a whiteboard on a wall with details of training schedules at the eight Nagpur centres. Two bound volumes of his PhD thesis sit on one shelf and the posters used in training sessions are rolled up and stacked on another table. He slides the windows shut to keep out the sound of music and celebrations.

Abhijeet is at work by 10 a.m. every day and spends the first two hours on email, the phone and administrative work. He then spends time with the coaches, getting feedback about what's happening at the local centres and making plans for the future. After lunch, when football sessions resume, he's back on the field visiting the different centres and watching the children and coaches at work.

Sessions are held twice a week for each group of twenty-five children. A session runs for an hour and a half, with the coaches infusing problem-solving and discipline into the football games. The equipment is left behind so that the children can get together and play whenever they want to. The premise is simple—football is the world's most popular game, and children need just a ball to get them going. 'No other sport generates as much passion and excitement. Yes, cricket in India, but cricket needs bats, stumps, wickets;

it's expensive, not everyone can play it,' says Abhijeet. 'You don't need a pitch or a great amount of skill to kick a ball around. And once they're playing, it's easy to transform their passion into meaningful skills.'

The coaches start by just playing with the children and slowly build a rapport with them. Once they start enjoying kicking a ball around, the rules of football are introduced. 'These kids have no concept of rules, so the football rules introduce them to order,' says Abhijeet.

Then, they start with things as simple as getting the children to cut their nails and comb their hair. Coming to a session on time and looking presentable is the start of lessons in discipline. 'We gently show them that just as there are rules in the game, outside too, in life, there are rules to follow. As you practise to get better and better at football, so too must you work hard at school. If you do things a particular way, you will improve.'

All of Slum Soccer's coaches are boys and girls who have been through its programmes, have played for India at the Homeless World Cup, and have been trained to lead the sessions that once helped them. The teenagers are now going to college and, supported by the non-profit, are doing undergraduate degrees in physical education, computer science, teaching, science and more. Slum Soccer has twenty-five coaches across the country, with four of the twelve in Nagpur working full-time for the programme. It has also started training teenagers to be leaders within their communities and impart education through football. 'Everyone here—working with us or taking part in the programmes—has a story,' says Abhijeet.

Since Slum Soccer's coaches are always from the community in which the centre is set up, the coach understands the problems and context of that slum. Parents are quicker to trust a familiar coach and send their children out to play. 'We draw the children in with football. Playing teaches them teamwork, fair play, inclusion, discipline. Then we use the rapport we have built to tackle a range of issues from education, peer pressure, conflict resolution and health to AIDS awareness, child abuse, crime and drug abuse,' says Homkant Surandase, who started playing in the zopadpatti football tournaments in 2005. 'We learn to make positive choices through football.'

Homkant holds himself up as an example of someone whose decision to play football changed his life. He ran away from his village in Maharashtra's Yavatmal district when he was fifteen because a number of farmers, faced with crushing debt, were taking their own lives. 'My father is a labourer and things were hard. I didn't want that life.' He came to Nagpur looking for Vijay Barse because he'd played in a zopadpatti tournament held in Yavatmal. 'I found him by chance in a slum, teaching a group of boys.' Homkant began training and represented India at the Homeless World Cup in Melbourne, Australia, in 2008.

The Homeless World Cup is a global social organization that promotes football among the underprivileged to encourage them to change their lives. They provide support and guidance in football and management skills to programmes like Slum Soccer. 'I loved the experience and met so many people from all over the world. So many languages and one game. They had achieved so much,' says Homkant. He has gone through the Homeless World Cup Foundation's programme for coaches, and works as a full-time coach with Slum Soccer and keeps an eye on all the centres. He's also doing an undergraduate degree in physical education in Nagpur. 'I want to tell everyone that they can see the world if they want to,' he says.

Abhijeet explains that such stories are easier to believe when the coaches themselves tell the children. The coach—be it Homkant, best female player Disha Lohabare, 2013 team captain Pankaj Mahajan or any of the twenty-five across the country—is a role model. 'The children love and look up to them. So when the coach tells them to stay away from drugs, they listen. It's better than someone else coming and lecturing them,' says Abhijeet.

One of the biggest challenges is sports being considered a competitor to education. 'Parents think sports is a waste of time. It is this mindset that we are trying to break, and having coaches from the community helps. Parents too slowly come to realize that sports can teach a lot about life,' he says.

Gender inclusion, for instance, is taught by tweaking the rules of the game a little—each team has to necessarily pick two female players, and the girls have to score a certain number of goals if the team wants to win. 'So the problem of boys leaving out the girls or refusing to pass the ball is sorted out. The girls are strong players and the boys see and recognize their contribution. It's a lesson they remember off the pitch too,' says Abhijeet. In red-light areas, games are used to teach awareness about AIDS and peer pressure. In orphanages, they usually have to tackle aggression and break up gangs. Coaches keep an eye on how children are doing at school.

'It's not like we have a tailor-made solution that we fit to the problem,' he says. Before they start a centre, Abhijeet spends weeks just observing and interacting with the children. 'That's where the skills from my education and research background come in handy.'

Once he lists the main problems, he and the coaches discuss what games and sessions to introduce to inculcate the kind of values the orphanage wants or the slum needs. He and the coaches try it; then the coaches take it to the field and bring him feedback. 'If it works, fine. If not, we have to change the game,' he says.

At the Koradi centre, the biggest in Nagpur with about 800 children, they're trying an experiment to integrate communities from the slum and housing colonies of local power plant employees. The children play together in mixed teams every evening. The economic differences are easy to spot from the shoes the players wear—the colony kids drift in slowly, discard expensive sneakers and don clean soccer boots, while the slum children race in pell-mell, kick off flip-flops and lace up second-hand boots or play in their black school shoes. But there's little else to differentiate them on the field as a good goal is a reason to cheer whether kicked in by a new boot or an old shoe. 'Over time, the on-field rapport will move off the field too,' Abhijeet says optimistically. 'Each centre presents a different challenge depending on the location and the professions and social and economic background of the parents.'

Abhijeet documents every step so that they know what works and what doesn't, and they don't have to start from square one if they encounter a similar situation again. The aim is to bring change through football. If the children are good enough, they play for India. If not, the coaches, along with Abhijeet and counsellors and psychologists who volunteer with Slum Soccer, identify non-football skills and prod the children in that direction. In Nagpur, for instance, Slum Soccer has tied up with a travel agency so that the older players can learn to work as tour guides. Another tie-up with wind turbine manufacturing company Gamesa has taken more centres and skilling programmes to children in villages near the company's plants as part of its corporate social responsibility initiative.

Abhijeet's main contribution is bringing an international perspective to the effort. 'I read a lot, experiment with ideas,' he says. When he started working with Slum Soccer in 2007, while teaching at Hislop College in Nagpur, the set-up was more informal without separate centres or a focus on life skills. 'I came in with the idea that I could mix education with the soccer tournaments my father was doing. Let's not do something for the sake of doing it but have an end result in mind,' he says.

He spoke with parents and learnt that the children had a more positive outlook after starting football and were less prone to getting into trouble. Watching the games, he realized the sessions could be used to talk about more than just football. He went online to see if it had been done before—Abhijeet had never been much of a football fan, preferring to follow basketball—and discovered that there were many organizations across the world using football for social change and that a whole world cup was played around the concept. 'I started planning to get us there in 2007.'

Abhijeet wrote to the Homeless World Cup (HWC), explaining what his father had been doing since 2001 and enclosed press clippings of articles the local media had done. HWC had heard of his father's work but had never been able to get in touch with him. They sent an invitation, and he put together a team for the 2007 tournament in Copenhagen. The first team didn't get too far but the players came back excited by what they'd seen and experienced, and were determined to share their stories and inspire others. 'It has been one of the biggest turning points for Slum Soccer. The children have a goal—they know that if they play well enough and exhibit certain qualities they can represent India,' says Abhijeet.

The returning team's spike in confidence opened his eyes to the real impact of football on children who'd had very little to look forward to in life. 'The change surprised even my father who had seen them play for so long,' he says.

But things were slightly less rosy on the home front. Abhijeet had got married earlier that year, and his wife Mahima wasn't very understanding of his obsession with street kids and football. 'She thought I was wasting my time,' he says. 'I felt I would make a difference.' Though she never restricted his work at Slum Soccer, the slight friction did make him second-guess himself. 'But I saw the change in the children and decided to carry on. My mother had resigned herself to me going the same way as my father.'

The next year, Abhijeet accompanied the team to Melbourne and realized that there were many others like them. He met people who were rehabilitating child soldiers, abused children, drug abusers, trafficked children, and more. All of them were using football for change—and receiving funding from international organizations like Street Football World and Homeless World Cup Foundation, something Krida Vikas Sanstha (KVS) was always short of.

He became aware of the fact that KVS needed to document its work and keep records if it was to attract large funding to keep programmes running smoothly instead of struggling along from one donation to the next. 'My father's vision was brilliant, but he followed trial-and-error methods. We needed a strategy,' he says. 'One man was doing the work of ten people. He put in his entire salary because he believed that he had enough to share with others. While I understand that, I felt we needed more money to reach more children,' he says.

The first thing he did was set up a separate football programme and rename it Slum Soccer, instead of zopadpatti football. 'If we wanted to grow and get international attention, we needed a catchier name that would stick easily in people's heads and mouths,' he says. After his trip to Melbourne, his wife, who works in the human resources department of a technology company, began making occasional trips to the centres to see what the fuss was about and slowly came around. 'Once the bigger projects started around 2009–10 and we started getting funding and grants, the last of her doubts disappeared. She supports herself, and I myself,' says Abhijeet.

He started work on the website, www.slumsoccer.org, and began writing to organizations across the world that were doing or supporting similar work. He reviewed projects and began winding up activities, such as tree-planting and blood donation camps, which took money but didn't show results. Programmes on employability, reproductive health and social awareness continue, with a clear vision of linking them to Slum Soccer.

In 2009, Slum Soccer got its first cheque from FIFA, which hosts the football world cup every four years. Since then, British club Tottenham Hotspur has come on board, followed by Street Football World. Nationally, Slum Soccer has received support from ONGC, Abhinav Bindra Foundation and Piramal Foundation. 'It's a more business-like approach, and I measure the social profit,' says Abhijeet.

Vijay is still the face of the organization in India, going into the slums to identify new spots for centres, being invited to functions as chief guest, making a push for sports as a nominated legislator in the Nagpur municipality council, and most recently being featured as a changemaker on the popular television show *Satyameva Jayate*, hosted by Bollywood actor Aamir Khan. He's also convinced the district administration to allow Slum Soccer to train municipal-school teachers to use football for education. 'People know me, and I like meeting them and talking about our work. Krida Vikas Sanstha has a new path as Slum Soccer. It's different from mine but it's going further than I could take it,' says Vijay, sitting in the portico of the pink building that he says will be his retirement home.

He and his wife, who recently retired as a physical education lecturer from a college in Chandrapur, plan to live on the ground floor with coaches Homkant, Umesh and Amol, who have practically adopted the Barses as family. Vijay points to the tiny garden he has started planting in front of the house and then walks round to the back to show off the trees that he is planting.

His only complaint is that his son does not spend enough time wooing the local media and sponsors and finds it easier to get support from abroad. 'It's always gratifying to be recognized in your own town no matter what the world thinks of you,' says Vijay,

Abhijeet's explanation is that raising money in India is harder since people do not seem to take sports very seriously. 'We've had people say they'd give us money if we switch to cricket. I always say no. Football is a world sport. It's cheap, easy, doesn't have too many rules, and there's more scope to experiment,' he says.

He's in the process of setting up different departments for fundraising and accounts, curriculum development, media, managing relationships with other organizations, and web presence, and has brought in volunteers to handle each aspect. They trained more than sixty young leaders—teenagers who will stand as examples within their community—in 2013, and are aiming to reach 100 in the next year. The Young Leaders programme began in 2013 to train coaches for the rapidly expanding Slum Soccer centres.

'It was getting hard to find coaches for our centres so I started a programme to train young people from the community to be leaders. It's my favourite programme in Slum Soccer because I literally see them find their voice,' says Abhijeet. Young people over sixteen can enrol for the programme where they acquire leadership skills, learn English, get communication and computer training, and are prepared for employment. 'They can either join us as coaches or go out and get jobs,' he says.

In 2014, the young leaders organized a Fairplay Football Tournament for ten rural teams in and around Nagpur as a test of what they had learnt. 'I was quite amazed at how well they managed without consulting the seniors at all,' says Abhijeet. That same year, he was selected for the year-long Acumen India Fellowship Programme to groom leaders making a significant social impact. Abhijeet is also trying to set up the US arm of Slum Soccer with the help of a few friends. 'Funding will become easier then,' he says.

At the end of 2009, three years after he moved back to India and started working with Slum Soccer, Abhijeet decided to drop his day job as a professor. 'I did a lot of introspection before I shifted. I did not jump in because I was not sure. I tried working two jobs for a long time,' he says. 'But, after a point, you have to commit to one.'

Until about four years ago, Abhijeet says he had nerve-wracking doubts about whether it had been sensible to abandon the safety of an academic career and a steady salary. He went without a salary for three years, and even now takes out very little, knowing that the money can be circulated within the programme. 'Even now there are days when nothing seems right and I doubt whether I have done the right thing,' he says. 'Then I get on to Skype and call one of the other mad people around the world who are doing what I do, and draw energy from them,' he says, laughing.

As for the impact he was seeking, Abhijeet says he can finally assess it. 'I can see that my efforts of the last five years have changed things—we are known globally for our work, we have supporters and funding, we have grown to forty centres across India working in slums, red-light areas, remand homes, we're working with children with different kinds of problems. Plus, there's a good feeling.'

ABHIJEET'S ADVICE

1. Start with very low returns on expectations.
2. Be familiar with the new field—you should know all the work that goes into it before you decide to do it.
3. Always run a stripped-down version of your idea before going full scale.

THE WAY INTO THE WILD

K. Ullas Karanth

One of the world's leading tiger biologists, K. Ullas Karanth started life as an engineer, switched to being a tractor salesman and then tried his hand at farming, before deciding to turn his lifelong love for nature into a career and retrain in his mid-thirties.

K. Ullas Karanth's mobile phone keeps ringing, an odd string of electronic beeps like a chirping bird that's in a contest with a chirruping cricket filling the room every few minutes. It's the call of that elusive bird, the Malabar Whistling Thrush. 'I'm sorry I can't put this on silent now. Mine is a crisis field,' he says, taking another call and speaking in Kannada. A forest officer was killed the night before by tourists, when he objected to them feeding crocodiles in the Kali river in the forests of Dandeli in Karnataka.

Karanth, one of the world's leading tiger biologists, is trying to garner some support for the officer—drafting letters to the government demanding action against the tourists, sending out press releases, and generally making a bit of a noise about the killing of a man who was just doing his job. He's in activist mode today in his office on Bangalore's busy Vittal Mallya Road, the jungle uniform of camouflage jacket and hat replaced by a black shirt and khaki trousers, phone in hand instead of binoculars. But it is in the forest surrounded by real birdsong and silently watching for all creatures great and small that he is happiest.

Karanth has spent much of the last forty years studying tiger behaviour as well as taking on the government—getting it to change the way it counts tigers, stopping mining in Kudremukh National Park, and melding science with activism to keep forests and wildlife safe. But he found his way to this path he truly loved only in his thirties. Before he retrained as a wildlife scientist, Karanth, now sixty-six, was by turn a mechanical engineer, a tractor salesman and a farmer.

Karanth's childhood was the seemingly ideal and wild one. Born in 1948 in Puttur, about 50 km from Mangalore, he didn't go to school till the age of eleven but spent most of his time watching birds and animals on the six-acre family property. 'My parents had very liberal ideas. My siblings and I didn't go to school till about class five; we just played all day. My mother taught us Kannada and a teacher some basic maths,' he says, looking out of the second-floor window. The simple office room he shares with his daughter and conservation biologist Krithi Karanth is lined with white shelves that hold volumes on predators, prey, animal behaviour, statistical modelling and writing and cat-themed bric-a-brac.

Books were Karanth's way into the world of wildlife. His father, celebrated Kannada writer Shivarama Karanth, had an extensive library with natural history books and copies of *National Geographic* magazine dating back to 1938, and an aunt gave him Salim Ali's book on birdwatching. He started watching birds when he was seven or eight, by which time the tiger already had him in its spell. 'I saw my first tiger in a circus and I was just fascinated. My father read Jim Corbett's books to me from a young age, and I would go to the forest nearby trying, in vain, to watch animals,' he says. 'Even today I may rationalize it as data models and all of that, but at the heart of it the connection to the tiger is very emotional.'

But when the time came to choose a career after he finished school in 1964, like most boys of that decade, he picked mechanical engineering at the National Institute of Technology, Karnataka, because 'you needed some job security'. Though his father suggested zoology, Karanth ignored him because he didn't want to end up as a doctor or a clerk. 'That was what happened to most zoology graduates in the 1960s,' he says. He wanted to work in the wild but didn't see a future in it and didn't know how to go about it.

Shikar writers such as Jim Corbett and Kenneth Anderson continued to feed his love for adventure and the forest, but it was a 1965 article by George Schaller in *Life* magazine that set him on the right track. Schaller, one of the world's foremost field biologists, had spent eighteen months in Kanha National Park, studying tigers. Unlike the colonial hunter-conservationists such as Corbett and Anderson whose approach was based solely on subjective experience, Schaller was clinical, focused and used objective scientific analyses to pose and answer specific questions relating to tiger behaviour and prey. 'He didn't just watch nature and make observations. He provided answers that were quantitative. It blew my mind. I realized this is what I should be doing,' Karanth says.

Inspired by Schaller, he took his motorcycle and headed off to the closest forest, which was Nagarahole wildlife sanctuary, just to watch animals and make notes the way Schaller had. Kudremukh became another favourite spot after he first went there in 1966, starting on the steep western side and trekking 20 km or more to the top. 'My third love is Bhadra, which I first visited in 1972. These were three places that I quite literally fell in love with,' he says. 'But I still didn't know how to make a living from this love. A career in wildlife was unheard of in those days.'

Since becoming India's Schaller seemed too far-fetched a dream, Karanth joined MICO, better known today as Bosch India, after graduating from engineering college in 1971. He calibrated diesel fuel injection pumps and designed parts for automated lathes. 'To me, the job was like being in jail for life. I called the factory "the concentration camp". All the signs and titles were in German. We worked from 7.45 a.m. to 5 p.m. every day,' he says. 'It was an extremely disciplined way of working and, on the bright side, I learnt that.'

After two years on the factory floor, he decided he'd had enough of being cooped up indoors and joined Agro Private Limited as a salesman for tractors, power tillers and other farm equipment. 'It wasn't much of a job but I got to travel all over Karnataka on my motorcycle to meet farmers and bank officers in rural areas. I would plan the field visits to end with a trip to a forest,' he says.

Being in the forests so often from his college days had brought him in contact with forest officers K.P. Achaiah and K.M. Chinnappa, both of whom taught him about wildlife, field craft and animal behaviour. 'I kept meticulous notes of all my observations,' he says. 'The more time I spent in the forest, the more I felt, "This is where I should be; why am I wasting time?"'

After three years as a tractor salesman, he bought forty-four acres of land near Nagarahole National Park, about 90 km from Mysore, and decided to give tobacco farming a shot. 'I told my wife, "Look, I'm thinking of giving up engineering and becoming a farmer." Ours was a love marriage, so we gave each other a lot of freedom. She said, "If you're sure it'll make you happy, I have no problem." So it was a quick decision to leave my job, take my savings, borrow some money from my father, and buy the farm, all in the hope of getting closer to nature,' he says.

Since his wife Prathibha, a speech pathologist, was planning to do a PhD, they moved from Bangalore to Mysore. He spent six days a week living in a mud-walled hut and growing tobacco near the small taluka town of Periyapatna, and went home on Sunday. 'Economically, it was very tough. Farming was hard—managing land and labour and coming to grips with local ideas of caste and power.' Karanth, rather influenced by Marxist ideas then, raised daily wages from Rs 2 to Rs 2.50. 'I thought I was doing the right thing but other farmers objected saying I was ruining them and tried to force the labourers to boycott me. Managing land makes you a rougher person; you have to change, otherwise you will sink,' he says.

Karanth spent eight years—from 1976 to 1984—as a farmer growing tobacco and a few other crops. 'I didn't enjoy the farming part but I enjoyed the fact that I could watch birds and be outdoors,' he says. Since farming only took up four months of the year, he was free to roam Nagarahole, spending time with Chinnappa, tracking and observing animals, picking up natural history skills, writing articles for Kannada papers on wildlife, watching for poachers in his neighbourhood and reporting them to the forest department.

Most of the poachers were from the villages surrounding Nagarahole. While the trade was not as organized or widespread as it is today, poachers were hunting for ivory, bone and meat, and villagers were grazing cattle, burning and stripping the forests for survival. 'Those years changed many of my idealistic, romanticized notions of rural harmony with nature,' he says. Karanth had initially been influenced by the writings of Madhav Gadgil, who argued that villagers are wise, traditional custodians of the forests with an inherent reverence for nature. Instead, he saw American ecologist Garrett Hardin's *Tragedy of the Commons* unfolding around him, where villagers stripped the forests for their immediate, individual benefits, unaware and unmindful of the long-term impact of their actions.

'Those years were instrumental in shaping my understanding of how humans relate to one another and to the forests that sustain us. The reason may be need or greed, but it's a scramble for resources and biomass in which people compete fiercely and end up harming the forest. I saw how strong an influence was caste, untouchability and social discrimination,' he says. They were lessons that would shape his head-and-heart approach of bringing science and practical application to conservation and forest management years later, a view that was often contrary to those held by most conservationists as well as the government.

In 1980, Karanth got involved in his first conservation campaign. Karnataka chief minister Gundu Rao invited Tiger Tops, a Nepal-based tourism company, to build a luxury lodge on the banks of Kabini River within the narrow corridor that connects the forests of Nagarahole to Bandipur. 'Hundreds of elephants congregate here in summer and the resort would have disrupted an important migratory path,' he says. So Karanth and a few friends began campaigning against the chief minister's pet project. He wrote articles in papers and tried to meet the chief minister.

When nothing came of that, he drafted a letter to the then Prime Minister Indira Gandhi explaining how the proposed resort would harm elephant ecology and migration and got his father and his writer friends, R.K. Narayan and U.R. Ananthamurthy, to sign it. 'R.K. Narayan was very interested in tigers because he had borrowed all my books and read them when he was writing *The Man-Eater of Malgudi*,' he says. 'After we sent the letter, I tracked down my father's friend H.Y. Sharada Prasad, who worked in the PMO, and nagged him every week till the letter was placed before the PM,' he says. Finally, Mrs Gandhi asked the chief minister to appoint an expert review committee. The committee looked at all the research Karanth had done and decided that the project should be shifted to a new location outside the forest, where it stands now, despite Rs 6 lakh being sunk into the foundation.

It was his first fight and Karanth was thrilled, but he also learnt that conservation is about using all available tools. 'It is like business or politics; you have to push the knife all the way in and do everything that is needed till you get there. Otherwise, you will fail,' he says. 'I was not a trained wildlife scientist at the time but I had done a lot of research to back up my demand. I still feel happy when I see the abandoned foundation in Mastigudi, overgrown with vegetation, surrounded by hundreds of elephants.'

Despite the experience he was gaining, those eight years on the land were a time of great self-doubt. 'I was learning but I can't say I was happy because every day was a struggle. We didn't have enough money, I was not enjoying farming. I was wondering what to do next, feeling sort of . . . stuck.'

A break came in the form of a Rotary Club Group Study exchange programme in the US in 1980, which he used as a chance to pick up the thread of the dream to become a wildlife biologist. After the programme, which involved travelling around the US to live with local families and meet opinion-makers, he went to the University of Wisconsin–Madison where Schaller had done his PhD. He explained to a professor in the wildlife department that he was an engineer turned farmer who now wanted to become a wildlife biologist.

'I was very apprehensive about being turned away but Professor McCabe was not at all surprised or annoyed. He explained that I could have any background to do a master's as long as I had a good GRE score and could convince the university that I was really interested in wildlife. He suggested that I publish some scientific papers,' says Karanth.

At thirty-two, he returned to India and dug out all the meticulous field notes he had kept for fifteen years while trying to emulate Schaller, and began writing. His first paper on Bhadra sanctuary was published by Bombay Natural History Society. A few months later, based on his research and publications, the Karnataka government gave him a grant of Rs 25,000 to do a survey of lion-tailed macaques. He discovered new populations of this rare monkey, and published the results in a reputed international journal. 'Once you publish, people read and get to know you,' he says.

Then he turned his attention to his favourite cat, the tiger. In the 1970s, the government had introduced the pugmark census method of counting tigers, based on the premise that each tiger has a unique track shape, which can be identified by officials. That first tiger census put India's tiger numbers at a definitive 1872, since foresters claimed to have traced and identified the pugmarks of every single tiger in the country. Karanth was sceptical; he knew the same tiger's tracks vary depending on soil, stride and speed of movement.

He used the government figures for tigers and prey, and did an analysis. 'I showed that you cannot have so many tigers with so little prey,' he says. This idea that prey determines the number of tigers an area can sustain would be one he would hone over the next few decades, doing studies and research in eleven reserves across the country, but it was close to twenty years before the Indian government acknowledged his findings and started using them to aid conservation.

Armed with this fieldwork and some publications, he headed to the centenary seminar of Bombay Natural History Society (BNHS) in Mumbai in 1983. In attendance were some of the world's leading wildlifers, including John Seidensticker and Mel Sunquist, who had finished an advanced tiger research project in Nepal. 'I latched onto Seidensticker and Sunquist, told them I wanted to be a tiger biologist, and showed them my analysis and all my work,' he says. 'I was very persistent. I wanted to convince them of my commitment and I did.'

They suggested the Smithsonian's three-month, intensive wildlife training programme for naturalists from developing countries. Karanth got accepted by the Smithsonian and spent part of 1984 in the US on the programme and with Sunquist at the University of Florida at Gainesville learning radio tracking and other skills before joining a postgraduate course. Back in India later that year, he gave up farming and started fieldwork in Nagarahole, studying tigers and their prey base, counting prey animals and analysing tiger scats and kills. He set up a non-profit wildlife research organization, Centre for Wildlife Studies (CWS), with his father-in-law and one of his tobacco buyers as the trustees, trying to raise funds for his work. 'I knew that if I was going to do this more systematically, I needed to put a framework in place. It was a very ambitious scheme—I wanted to do wildlife research in India,' he says. Since then, CWS has grown to become an organization that covers wildlife research, education and conservation.

Karanth did things backwards—he didn't join college, do his coursework and then his fieldwork like most students. Instead, he collected all his data for his dissertation and then joined the University of Florida in 1987 under Sunquist's supervision, and finished the next year. 'I did well. For the first time, I actually enjoyed classes. I was thirty-eight-plus while most of the students were bright, young Americans, but I was more focused and had a lot of experience,' he says, his voice mellowing with the memories. 'It was really fun. The hardest thing was typing; you had so many assignments and I had never learnt typing.'

Karanth blossomed in what was then the best wildlife school in the US, making friends with seniors and juniors who would go on to become leaders in the field, and attending classes taught by top conservation scientists. For the first time, he felt confident he could make a success of his professional life.

'I've never regretted quitting any of my old jobs because I never particularly enjoyed them. I was an average engineer simply because I was not interested. I was not a rich farmer because there were other things that interested me more,' he says. 'I knew that the going would be tough as a tiger biologist, but it was what I wanted to do so I never doubted the fact that I would do well.'

Towards the end of the academic year, his hero Schaller visited the university and Karanth, the best student, made a presentation. After the presentation, he told a sceptical Schaller that he wanted to return to India and study tigers. 'He didn't believe me. In those days, most Indians never came back. Life there meant a car, life here meant a motorcycle; the differences were very stark,' he says. 'I told him I will go back because I want to write a tiger book that would be better than his,' says Karanth, chuckling. 'I haven't done that yet, I still have time.'

Schaller took a liking to the outspoken Karanth and asked him to visit the Wildlife Conservation Society (WCS) headquarters in New York after he finished his course. Schaller's WCS gave Karanth a stipend for research, and he began radio-collaring tigers in Nagarahole in October 1989. His was the first radio telemetry study on tigers in India, and the second in the world. Radio telemetry involves tranquillizing an animal, fitting it with a radio collar, and following it over the next few years to study its behaviour.

Getting a degree and a project was just the start. He now had to prove himself in a field that was just emerging in India and at a time when the thrust was on development. 'Are animals more important than humans?' was the standard question asked when conservation issues came up against commercial interests.

'The local vested interests opposed my research totally,' he says. Karanth hadn't realized that his years of working with Chinnappa to protect Nagarahole from poachers, loggers, cattle grazers and corrupt officials had raised so many hackles. All tiger deaths during that period were attributed to Karanth, his tranquillizers and collars. '1990 was the worst year,' he says. Six tigers died in Nagarahole between March and July 1990—one was a twelve-year-old male tiger, one was poached, and four died in intraspecific fights. Only the aged male was a collared animal, but rumours started—and persisted—that they were dying of the after-effects of the tranquillizers. The accusations continued despite the fact that the collaring had been done in January and the tigers had died after March. 'I have a huge file of all those crazy, libellous press cuttings from that time,' he says.

Karanth's research was stopped, so he went to court. 'I came back in 1991. By then some of the animals had lost the collars. I continued out of persistence but every time a tiger or a leopard died in Nagarahole it would be attributed to me. I became the tiger killer. It was awful,' he says. Finally in 1993, the government accepted an expert committee's enquiry report that absolved him of all blame. It was also the year that he finished his PhD from Mangalore University.

WCS offered him a full-time position as an Assistant Conservation Scientist but he hesitated. He was concerned that a foreign NGO would be too politically correct and would not want to take a controversial stand on anything. 'I liked my freedom, but they convinced me to join them and it's worked out well. I've got into all sorts of trouble with the government—nothing illegal of course—but we have gone head-to-head with the government and anti-wildlife forces many times, when it means choosing what is best for the wildlife,' he says.

The good thing that came of the struggle against the opposition to his research is that he became quite impervious to personal attacks, growing a thick skin that would serve him well later on. 'I was trained as a scientist and my father was a writer so the kind of crass politicking that I came up against during the telemetry project was new to me,' he says. 'It was very upsetting.'

Sometime in 1991, when then Karnataka chief minister S. Bangarappa came to Nagarahole, Karanth managed to get a meeting with him and explain the problems he was facing in the forest and the way he was being slandered. 'All he said was "you have to develop a hide like a water buffalo if you are committed to something and want to do whatever it is you want to do." It is advice I took to heart and now all these things don't bother me though they still keep happening,' he says.

In 1996, he decided to change the direction of his tiger project and move on. 'I had one tigress left whom I had tracked for six years and had learnt a lot about tiger behaviour, but it was unbelievable the amount of stress I had to undergo,' he says. 'What kept me going was the fact that I had finally found what I wanted to do.'

Since the emerging national crisis at that time was the sharp drop in tiger numbers due to poaching for the Chinese medicine trade, he decided to look at new, reliable ways to estimate tiger populations. As a graduate student, Karanth had gone to a conference and seen 'camera traps' used as aids for hunting. He thought the same concept—hunters using automatic cameras to identify antlered bucks to shoot later—could be used to count tigers. Since each tiger has a unique stripe pattern, almost like human fingerprints, photographing and creating a database of identified tigers would be a good way to estimate their numbers, he reasoned.

It's a simple system—a point-and-shoot camera is connected to a tripping device and set up on a forest path. A tiger walking on the path triggers the camera, which takes its picture. The stripe patterns are compared later, and the tigers counted.

He had studied statistical modelling, and worked with leading quantitative ecologist James D. Nichols in the US to develop sampling methods for wildlife. 'So started the great synergy between my quantitative education and my love for carnivore biology. I was not afraid of numbers and statistics like many biologists,' he says. 'Twenty years later, I finally appreciated my engineering background.'

Karanth and Nichols developed methodologies that meshed camera data with sophisticated statistical models to estimate the tiger population. By 1996, when the radio telemetry project was winding down, WCS gave Karanth a mandate to build a tiger programme across India. 'I had started questioning the accepted methodology more than a decade earlier. Now I had the answer: using camera-trapping and these statistical models. I shifted the focus of my research to population studies from individual behaviour studies. I felt this was far more useful for conservation. After all, you can't change a tiger's behaviour but tiger numbers are critical.'

Karanth's pioneering camera traps and modelling and estimation tools have opened up many avenues for understanding tigers and have been adopted worldwide for other big cats such as jaguars and leopards. 'I started experimenting with camera traps in 1991 and by 1993, I knew they worked well. The Indian government started using them only in 2005. It took them twenty-five years to acknowledge that the pugmark method was rubbish,' says Karanth, who is now the director for Science-Asia at WCS.

Gradually the recognition also came—Sierra Club's EarthCare award in 2006, WWF's J. Paul Getty Award in

2007, the Fellowship of the Indian Academy of Sciences in 2008, the Karnataka government's Rajyotsava award in 2011, and in 2012, the Padma Shri from the Government of India for outstanding contribution to wildlife conservation and environment protection. He has helped research and conservation projects in Thailand, Malaysia, Cambodia, Myanmar, Indonesia, Russia, and Africa and Latin America.

In the last couple of years, Karanth has been spending less time in the forest and more time guiding younger researchers and volunteers to ensure that tigers continue to roam free in the Malenad landscape in which he grew up. He is an advisor to a number of advocacy groups started in the early 1990s to protect wildlife in Karnataka and whose conservation philosophy is similar to his own. Among their bigger victories are the resettlement of more than 1000 families from forests in Karnataka and shutting down the biggest iron ore mine in Kudremukh, which was destroying forests and rivers.

All through these fights, Karanth and his conservation partners had to face smear campaigns, all because of their uncompromising stand. He is neither one of the greens who stands on the outside, holds protests and refuses to listen to government reasoning nor the garden variety of NGO worker or scientist who is afraid to criticize the government and lose consequent benefits and access to the forest. 'We support or oppose the government based on the issue at hand,' he says.

His demands for conservation action are always underpinned by strong science and research, a sort of head-and-heart approach that hasn't always gone down well with the activist community, other scientists or the government. 'I've pushed really hard and gone against the grain of the conservation community by advocating separation of tigers from humans. Not by kicking people out of the forest, which was the standard government model earlier, but by giving them a better deal and advocating voluntary resettlement,' he says.

Looking back on a forty-year career of protecting the wilds from the urban jungle, Karanth says he's more convinced than ever of the WCS mandate to protect wildlife and wild lands across the world. 'These are places I love—Nagarahole, Kudremukh and Bhadra—and I've had a role in doing something beneficial for them by coming up with a few ideas that work on the ground,' he says. 'My work is not just about saving these magnificent creatures. There is a kind of fulfilment I get from being there. I just love what I do.'

TIPS TO FIND THE RIGHT PATH

1. If you really love something, you should not be afraid to switch. The only reason you should leave one career for another is if you are truly passionate about the new one. Otherwise, you will find yourself in the same soup.

2. A good knowledge of natural history is essential for those who want to pursue a career in wildlife biology, conservation and related areas. Without on-ground knowledge, it's hard to be effective and understand the real concerns. And that's true of any profession.

3. However passionate you are about animals, always be guided by science. Saving a species is more important than trying to save every individual of that species. Shooting a man-eater quickly is necessary to save other living tigers and their habitats with local support. Be practical.

UP IN THE AIR

Rahul Devesher

After four years as a media planner and twenty-odd years of dreaming of flying, Rahul Devesher spent four years in flight school and became a pilot with a commercial airline.

There are eight minutes that Rahul Devesher will never forget. And one shirt that he will never throw away. The minutes he spent up in the air, flying a plane solo for the first time, and the shirt he was wearing on that flight.

He pulls up a photograph of the shirt on his phone. It's covered with writing, the congratulatory scrawls of friends, instructors and staff at his flying school. The rather unremarkable shirt is a reminder of Rahul's long and often lonely journey from media planner to pilot.

'You sense that the day of your solo is near after you've trained for close to two years, but you don't know when it will be,' he says, looking at the photograph closely as if he

163

needs to remember every scribble. 'The instructor took me out as usual and after the third practice run, he said, *"Kar lega?"* meaning "will you manage?" Of course!'

The instructor informed Air Traffic Control that he was sending a student out on his first solo. 'So I went. I was so focused on doing everything right that it didn't sink in. Those few minutes felt like hours. It's only after I landed and did all the checks that I felt the exhilaration. It's still like that; while I'm in the air, there's so much to keep track of that I don't feel anything. On land, I'm thrilled to be flying for a living,' he says.

Rahul is a captain with IndiGo airlines, which he joined in January 2015 after more than six years with Jet Airways, where he started as a trainee, flew as first officer for four years and finally made it to captain. It's the realization of a dream he kept alive for twenty-odd years through school in tiny villages and towns across the country, colleges in Bhopal and Ahmedabad, and four years of work as a media planner.

'All I wanted to do was fly planes but it seemed like an impossible dream,' he says, relaxing in his hotel room in Chennai after a delayed flight from Bangalore. Rahul is a reedy guy with rimless glasses, an unassuming manner, and a touch of languid boredom. 'We were number eighteen to land today. Traffic up there is just as bad as down here. We got from Bangalore to Chennai in twenty minutes, but spent an hour over the sea waiting to land. We went halfway to Port Blair and came back,' he says.

Rahul's plans to be a pilot were made at the age of eight when he saw fighter jets on TV during a Republic Day parade. 'I wanted to fly them,' he says. 'I suppose every boy wants to but for me planes became an obsession. I lived in a tiny town where I saw about three cars a day—now I get stuck in traffic jams and air traffic jams all the time, but that's another point. Back then, the idea of people flying was unbelievable.'

Rahul was born in Jalandhar in Punjab in 1977 and grew up in Kamalapuram and Warangal in Andhra Pradesh, Chandrapur district in Maharashtra and Yamunanagar in Haryana where his father's jobs took the family. 'Before I discovered planes, I'd been fascinated by trains and wanted to be an engine driver. I'd always liked things with wheels—cars, trains, then planes.'

In the era before the Internet and affordable books, Rahul clipped out pictures and articles about civil and military aircraft from newspapers and magazines and turned them into posters to paper the walls of his room. 'The pride of my collection was a big article that came out when Air India bought its first Boeing 747-400 in the early 1990s,' he says. 'I knew the specs of all the planes by heart even though I'd never travelled in one.'

When people asked him what he wanted to do for a living, he caused a lot of amusement by saying 'pilot'. 'No one believed me. If you said anything other than doctor or engineer, you were mad. They'd laugh and say, "Okay, but what do you really want to be?"'

After he finished class ten in 1993, the family moved to Bhopal and Rahul went to junior college. In class twelve, he applied to the National Defence Academy to join the Air Force but didn't get through because he wore glasses and was underweight. 'I was even skinnier then. I touched 50 kg only last year. So I thought that dream was over. The NDA was the only place I knew of where they taught you to fly planes.'

His hopes rose when he saw an ad in the newspaper for a flying school near Chennai. He pored over the prospectus the school sent him and was excited to read that the fee for the commercial pilot course was Rs 50,000. 'I showed it to my dad and told him that was where I wanted to study after school. He looked at me strangely and said, 'I only own a scooter and you want to learn to fly planes for five lakhs?' I looked at it again—I had read the zeros wrong. I quickly apologized and threw the prospectus away. Five lakhs was too large an amount to consider.'

With that he gave up entirely on the dream of becoming a pilot. 'I lost my way after that. I was not interested in anything else,' he says. Rahul, who had been a good student, started getting into trouble and bunking classes. 'Everything seemed like a waste. The only thing that appealed to me was not working out. I couldn't bring myself to find a new direction. It caused a lot of tension at home,' he says.

Rahul failed class twelve, which shook him up. He repeated his exams, passed in 1996 and enrolled for a BA in English and Economics at a local college. 'I wasn't particularly interested in the course but Bhopal was a nice city and English was a subject I liked.' He enrolled for a computer course at NIIT, and at the Alliance Française for French. 'I was not really serious about a career but went with the crowd, doing the things other students did. In my final year, I put in the application forms for MBA entrance tests since everyone else was doing it,' he says. An acquaintance at NIIT was filling in a form for Mudra Institute of Communications, Ahmedabad (MICA) and Rahul did the same. 'I took the CAT (Common Admission Test for entrance to the IIMs) without any real hope. I really didn't have a plan for my life, for anything,' he says.

He got admission to an MBA course in a local Bhopal college and was quite cheerfully looking forward to whiling away another two years in a city that is pleasantly green with lots of lakes and parks. A month or so later, he got an email asking him to appear for an interview at MICA. He then went online and did some reading and realized that MICA is one of the country's best mass communication institutes. 'I joined MICA in 2000, and I loved it. I ended up there by chance but it was such fun—the students, the classes, the professors, the environment . . . I enjoyed myself,' he says.

The shifts from obscure villages that are hard to pinpoint on Google Maps to cities had progressively widened his horizons. Ahmedabad was the largest city he had lived in and he met people from across the country with a variety of interests. 'I was learning every day. Then we went to Bombay for the summer internship in 2001. I loved it, my first experience of a big city,' he says.

He no longer thought about being a pilot, but being in a stimulating environment rekindled his love for aviation. 'Theatre, film, history . . . people had so many different hobbies. MICA was a place where it was okay to be different, to be passionate about something to the point of being crazy,' he says. Free access to the Internet helped him build his knowledge about planes, geography and aviation history. When students were asked to create presentations on topics of their choice, Rahul always chose aviation-based themes. 'My classmates and professors still remember those presentations. In MICA, planes became a full-fledged hobby,' he says.

After college, he joined Grasim Cement's marketing division in 2002 and a year later moved to Mindshare, a media planning agency in Mumbai, where several of his classmates worked. 'My life was going on. My bosses were fun; it was a casual work atmosphere. I was earning well. I was good at my job so I enjoyed it. When you do something over a period of time, you learn what works best and you fall into a pattern.'

For Diwali in 2002, he bought plane tickets for himself and his sister to fly from Mumbai to Chennai to visit their parents who were posted there. 'It was my first time on a plane. Air India, Airbus A310,' he says. 'I saw everything up close, felt the sensation of taking off, of landing. It was all so exciting. I wanted to be in the seat up front.'

The short flight had awakened his childhood dream. 'The idea that you could leave your job and find another life suddenly came to me,' he says. At Mindshare three colleagues who had been in his class at MICA quit to study in the US. A few seniors had left jobs to set up their own companies, pursue their love for theatre or take up other interesting careers. 'I had grown up with the idea that once you start working, that's it. You don't leave your career. Here, my friends were leaving good jobs to be students again and they were happier for it.'

He'd sit in his chair staring at the wallpaper on his monitor—the cockpit of a plane—and wonder if all he wanted to do for the rest of his working life was plan advertising strategies for shampoos and diapers. 'I could see the boss's glass cabin if I rolled my chair a bit,' he says, rolling the chair he's sitting on and craning his neck. 'Do I want to be there five to ten years from now? No,' he says.

British pilot and author Clive Hughes' book, *Guide to Becoming a Professional Pilot*, gave him more information and he began toying with the idea of getting a private pilot licence (PPL). Towards the end of 2003, a friend introduced him to a pilot she knew and he gave Rahul tips about preparing for the preliminary exams as well as flying schools he could enrol in.

'I had packed away that dream, but being in Mumbai revived it. I had access to all the information I lacked before, and had friends who had decided to try new things despite holding good jobs. Having a bit of financial security also gave me the confidence that I could give it a shot,' Rahul says.

He confided in his mother but kept his father out of the loop. 'My father was very angry with me for having left Grasim, a Birla company, to join Mindshare. He thought Grasim was a stable, reliable company and I should have retired from there. So I didn't tell him that I was considering quitting Mindshare as well. I didn't want to bring up being a pilot again.' His father believed that it was Rahul's up-in-the-air pilot dreams that had ruined his school days and the reason why he had failed class twelve. 'So I decided I would tell him later, maybe after I had finalized my plans,' he says.

Rahul made a trip to Ahmedabad Aviation and Aeronautics (AAA), which the pilot friend had recommended, to make enquiries about getting a PPL for a fee of Rs 2 lakh. They gave him a joyride in a Cessna 152, a two-seater propeller aircraft, the plane in which he would have to do sixty hours to get a PPL. 'The first time I sat in that aircraft I was damn scared. It's unpressurized so you can hear all the noise; you can feel the air coming at you. It's like a kite, the way it wiggles in the air.'

As the flight progressed, he settled down and began to think he could actually learn to fly it and enjoy it. The AAA staff told him about the Commercial Pilot Licence (CPL) which cost Rs 9 lakh, required 200 hours of flying, and would make him eligible for a full-time job. He flew back to Mumbai with his head in the clouds.

He decided to settle for a PPL which he could do while working and pay for himself. He took the written PPL test but failed it. 'I thought they would ask questions about aircraft specifications, aviation history and geography so it was an eye-opener sitting for the exam and realizing that mere love for the subject was not going to get me through.'

The PPL required cramming subjects such as air navigation, air meteorology and air regulation, which were mandatory for CPL applicants too. 'The initial idea was just to learn to fly a plane so that I would not have regrets thirty years down the line. Two things made me choose the CPL: one, I would be preparing for it anyway while studying for the PPL; and two, I did not want to be sitting at a desk five years later,' he says.

His bosses supported his decision to chase down the licence and said his job would be waiting should he want to return. His mother gave him the money she had inherited from her mother. Rahul quit Mindshare in December 2004. 'It was a fun decision. Until then, I had just played the cards life had dealt me. This time, I was adventurous.'

When his father found out Rahul had quit to sink his mother's savings into flight school, he was livid. 'Rahul and his mother had a whispering campaign and I was not involved at all. It was a terrible, terrible shock to me,' says Govind Devesher over the phone from Delhi. 'I wanted him to have a cushy, nine-to-five job. After all the uncertainty of his eleventh and twelfth, I was grateful he had settled down. He told me only after he had quit; there was nothing for me to do but sulk. I was very disappointed and told him so.'

Rahul moved to Ahmedabad and started his flying lessons in 2005. 'Reality hit me hard. There was so much to study. I was in a class filled with students who were straight out of school because the basic qualification is a pass in class twelve with physics and maths as subjects. At twenty-eight, I was one of the oldest,' he says.

For the first few months, the lessons were purely theoretical. About eight months after he joined flight school, flying lessons began and his solo came two or three months later. Practical training started with familiarizing oneself with the plane and practising circuits—just taking off and landing—for fifty to sixty hours. After the first solo circuit on 3 December 2005, which earned Rahul his graffiti-ed shirt, it was time for cross-country flying with an instructor, going from one point to another navigating with a map. Thirty hours of flying with just instruments followed, and another twenty-four hours of night flying before the instructor deemed him ready to take the test conducted by the Directorate General of Civil Aviation to earn a CPL.

Since most flying schools have more students than aircraft, getting up in the air takes a while. 'Often, you get just thirty minutes in four days. After my solo, for instance, I didn't get a plane for six days. The exhilaration of the flight dips when you have to wait so long,' he says of the two years he spent in flight school. 'A lot of it is just waiting— for a plane, for an instructor to fly with you, for ATC clearance, for clear weather, for the results from DGCA. It's very lonely because people are at various stages of training and it's hard to make friends. It wasn't like MICA where we were all in it together,' he says.

Another heart-rending lesson was that passion alone isn't enough. For Rahul, being a pilot was not about getting another job, it was about a dream coming true. On the ground and in the air, though, he had to contend with younger, more talented learners who were quicker to grasp the skills. 'You love something so much but once you're actually doing it, you find that other people are better than you. They don't have much passion but they are gifted. It's an art to fly. It's hard to realize that passion is not enough.'

It was only after he did his first cross-country solo flight and he could fly the aircraft on his own that the cloud of disillusionment lifted. 'The joy of flying, or rather knowing that you can fly, keeps you going.'

Rahul got his licence, a blue-rexine-covered booklet that looks like a passport, in May 2007 and two months later joined Sahara Airlines, which later became JetLite. 'There have been a few "highs" in my life: that letter from MICA, the first solo, and landing a first officer's job,' says Rahul.

His father came around slowly after he got his certificate. 'I had been worried because flight school had been a painful experience for him, but when he called to say he'd qualified, it was like a fairy tale. Who would have believed it could happen? I am more comfortable with it now,' says Govind.

Eight more months of training followed to upgrade him from a 200-hour, propeller-engine pilot to the co-pilot of a commercial Boeing 737 jet. 'The jump is crazy. You are just not prepared for it. The concept is the same: wings make you fly, engines give you power, but commercial passenger flying is all about management. There are so many different systems on board—two jet engines, hydraulics, pressurization, avionics, automation, flight management computer, routes and airways, fuel, radios and more. And with passengers and cargo, managing weight and balance and making weather-related evaluations can be difficult if your only experience is in a Cessna,' he says, pulling up another photograph of the many panels with knobs and buttons that surround him in the cockpit. A trainer aircraft has just one engine, basic instrumentation for altitude and speed, and one more seat. A Cessna flies at about 100 km per hour, a jet lands at 200 km per hour. 'Commercial flying is a choreographed dance. Every guy has procedures to follow and you can't put a step out of line. It was like starting from zero again.'

In March 2008, Rahul completed the mandatory hours of simulator training, observation flying and practice runs in India and the UK, and was released as a first officer. 'My first commercial flight was from Delhi to Bangalore. It took three whole years of pain for the joy of that nearly-three-hour flight. As usual, I was quite nervous and felt good only after touching down.'

By the end of 2012, he had been made captain. In a sense, it's the end of the line because there are just two promotions in this field—from trainee to first officer and then to captain. Skill development and training continues for life since DGCA makes pilots take practical and written tests every six months to ensure that they are air-worthy in every way. He is currently training to make the shift from Boeing to Airbus aircraft after the move to IndiGo in January 2015. 'It'll be about two months before I get into a proper flight.'

Though commercial flying can be demanding, Rahul is sure he has made the right choice. And every now and then, he does a quick check. 'I look up at the sky whenever I hear a plane and I feel that little thrill, the excitement of trying to identify the make,' he says. 'My passion is still intact.'

RAHUL'S TIPS TO FLY HIGH

1. Don't give up on a dream. I just kept thinking it could happen. Somehow staring at a plane's cockpit every day on my desktop helped me do something to make it a reality.
2. There will be hurdles. The important thing is not to get pulled down by them.
3. Learn as much as you can. Knowledge and passion are important. I didn't have access to much in the small towns I grew up in but devoured every bit of information about planes that I came across. Now with the Internet, it's so easy to inform yourself about subjects you're interested in.

GIVING PARLIAMENT
A LITTLE PUSH
M.R. Madhavan

Former financial markets analyst M.R. Madhavan is co-founder of a non-profit research initiative that provides data and information to people and politicians, empowering them to ask the right questions and demand better governance.

Every Thursday morning, M.R. Madhavan heads to a flat-fronted building about five minutes from Parliament House in New Delhi. The letters on the roof spell Constitution Club of India, an establishment set up in February 1947, before Independence, where the framers of the Constitution would relax after a hard day of debating the nuances of governing a yet-to-be-formed nation. More than sixty-eight years later, Members of Parliament (MPs) meet in its conference room to discuss and analyse bills that are to be taken up the following week. Former currencies expert Madhavan and his team from the non-profit research initiative PRS Legislative Research spend an hour with the MPs discussing the key features of the bill, going through the clauses, and helping the legislators understand the nuances and implications of each so that they can come to an independent and informed decision on whether to support or oppose the bill when it is taken up for debate and vote in Parliament. The discussions are detailed and analytical with neither the team nor the MPs taking partisan positions.

The main force behind this open yet closed-door forum for MPs is Madhavan, who spent ten years as a financial markets analyst before putting those same skills to use in the not-for-profit sector. PRS Legislative Research, which he co-founded, is an impartial research cell to support MPs and MLAs across party lines with background research on legislative and policy issues as well as provide data to citizens so that they can ask their representatives the right questions and demand better governance. The idea is to strengthen the working of the most important government institutions—Parliament and state legislatures. 'We're trying to fix some problems in our democratic systems,' says Madhavan. 'Everyone in India talks about improving governance but no one wants to put their money where their mouth is.'

Since it was set up in 2005, New Delhi-based PRS has summarized hundreds of unwieldy bills to a couple of pages of easy reading, provided background research for parties, and helped the media buttress its reports with data. Ahead of the 2014 Lok Sabha polls, election websites of Google, NDTV and *Malayala Manorama* linked to PRS's portal to provide information on candidates. The data on the site, www.prsindia.org, ranges from attendance of MPs and summaries of bills to updates on parliamentary discussions and compilations of state laws.

'People need to learn more about their government and how it works. They want better governance but don't know how to demand it. We're trying to put as much information as we can online because someone wanting to learn about legislative policy should not be hampered by lack of information, or put off by long documents,' Madhavan says. In January 2013, for instance, a PRS team took one day to shrink the much-awaited, 630-page Justice Verma Committee Report recommending amendments to the criminal law to two pages and upload it on its website along with the full text. The Committee had been formed after the Nirbhaya gang rape in New Delhi in December 2012 pushed civil society on to the streets demanding quicker justice and harsher punishment for those accused of sexual assault. The committee made recommendations on laws related to rape, sexual harassment, trafficking, child sexual abuse, medical examination of victims, police, electoral and educational reforms. Painstaking research, collating data and rewriting may not seem exciting to most but they put a sparkle in the eye of Madhavan, a genial, bespectacled forty-something, with close-cropped hair, a shy yet quick smile and a slight squint, who cheerily counters any questions about his work being ponderous with, 'Oh, but I find it very exciting, the idea of every citizen being able to get whatever information he or she wants.'

When it comes to MPs, the idea is to arm them with information that would enable them to make better decisions. During each of the three Lok Sabha sessions in a year, an MP can be confronted with up to sixty bills. The subjects can range from water, pension and taxation to introducing criminal amendments and anti-corruption laws. 'The MP is expected to understand the nuances of each of these diverse subjects and frame an appropriate law, apart from holding the existing government accountable and asking questions. The expectations are fair since we've elected them, but are the MPs equipped to do all this? Where are their qualified staff and research resources?' asks Madhavan. 'Imagine if you had to run a company without any competent, qualified staff or knowledge; that's precisely what our MPs are doing.'

Abroad, most legislators have entire teams working for them, putting together data, statistics, precedents, and all sorts of information that feeds into their debates, presentations and speeches. The Congressional Research Service based within the US Library of Congress, for instance, has more than 600 employees who provide independent research and background information to all members, regardless of party affiliation. In the UK, about 100 people in the Houses of Commons and Lords support members. In contrast, MPs in India neither have a culture of hiring research teams nor do they have peers and advisors who provide impartial information. That's the gap he set out to fill when he started PRS in 2005 with his friend C.V. Madhukar.

For ten years, Madhavan had worked as a strategist, researching international currency movements in relation to various sectors of the economy, and writing papers on them for banks across the world. 'You try to predict what factors affect the rupee and interest rates, and decide whether the client should buy or sell,' he says. 'It's a challenge and there was a thrill in getting it right,' says Madhavan, whose last corporate job was as senior strategist, Asian currency markets, at Bank of America in Singapore.

Research and analysis has always interested Madhavan, who was born in 1968 and went to school in New Delhi and Palghat in Kerala. He studied mechanical engineering at IIT Madras from 1986 to 1990 before going to IIM in Kolkata (IIM C) for an MBA, which he finished in 1992. 'Everybody did engineering and management, so I did it too. I didn't particularly love it or hate it,' he says.

He discovered his love for quantitative analysis and operations research in college and joined the production systems team in Maruti Udyog's IT department in 1992. The next year, he went back to IIM C for a PhD fellowship programme, which he finished in November 1995, and took a job with ICICI Securities in Mumbai. 'I worked there till 2000 doing research on equities and interest rates,' he says. He and Madhukar were billeted together at a company flat in Mumbai and hit it off. They would have long discussions on their jobs and how research could be linked to governance. 'I got intrigued and started reading and thinking about these issues. I found out that most advanced democracies had invested heavily in providing research support to national legislators. I was surprised and appalled that India had not done so,' he says.

Madhukar soon left the corporate world and joined educational NGO Pratham and later moved to Azim Premji Foundation but the two stayed in touch. Madhavan got involved with Pratham as a volunteer in its early days, and had many discussions on governance with its co-founder Madhav Chavan. 'Madhav and Madhukar have inspired me in many ways,' he says. Though the idea of contributing positively to society intrigued him, Madhavan stayed in the corporate world and moved to Bank of America in Mumbai in 2000.

'My clients were mostly corporates and hedge funds. I did research to predict how the dollar would move in relation to the rupee,' he says. Early in 2004, he moved to the bank's Singapore office to make the same predictions for other world currencies. He was one of three people in the company doing what he did and reported to the sector head in New York. 'There was a lot of writing and analysis in my work and I enjoyed it.'

When they were chatting sometime in 2002, Madhukar suggested setting up a research cell to support MPs. 'I was enticed by the idea,' he says. The fact that he and his colleagues were paid extremely well was proof that fund managers were finding research analysis valuable. Why wouldn't MPs, who have a far more important and challenging job, find it useful too? 'For Parliament to function well, research inputs are necessary,' he says.

No one in India was doing policy research for MPs at that time. 'The more I thought about it, the better the idea seemed. I don't have the emails from that time but Madhukar and I talked about it a lot. We both had the skills we had honed at our jobs—how to do research and extract the essentials, how to present the research simply and correctly—and were unbiased,' says Madhavan. After a year in Singapore, Madhavan realized ennui had set in. He enjoyed work but wasn't particularly excited by it. The concept of making information on governance comprehensible and accessible, on the other hand, consumed him. 'For me, the romance is in the fact that decisions which affect us all and have the potential to change the lives of millions of people for the better are made in Parliament in a deliberative consensual manner—at least in theory,' he says. 'Our parliamentary system is extremely inclusive and democratic. Anyone has the right to raise objections or offer insights on any bill being tabled in Parliament. It's just that there is a procedure for it and people are unaware of this.' He discussed the idea with different groups and think tanks over the course of a year, and got a great deal of encouragement. 'But given that we had never interacted with the target audience—MPs— the plan was a leap of faith. We thought that if we give a high-quality product, there would be users,' he says.

Making the decision to leave his job was not difficult. 'I switched careers because the idea was enticing and I was a bit bored with my old career. I had a good education and nothing to fear. My previous role was only to make hedge funds and their clients richer. That is essential too because it keeps the economy growing, but this is socially relevant and it makes me satisfied,' he says. Madhavan, who is single, set himself a two-year period to revisit the decision, confident that with his experience he would easily be able to re-enter the investment banking world. 'I had no liabilities and enough savings to take care of any medical contingencies for my mother or me. I think we exaggerate the risks of switching lines,' he says. 'There was nothing to lose, and possibly, some fun to be had. It's been close to ten years with PRS and I have no regrets at all.' He was comfortably off but planned his exit from the corporate world. He resigned in March 2005, after the year's bonus was paid, and took off on a six-month backpacking trip around Indonesia and India. 'I had worked without a long break. I went to Himachal Pradesh, Ladakh . . . parts of India I'd never seen before. It was a wonderful experience and taught me so much about my country,' he says.

Towards the end of his trip in September, he found himself in a railway station in Sanchi, where a man settled on to a bench beside him. 'We got talking and he asked me what I did. I said I had worked in a bank and had resigned. He told me that he too worked in a bank. He earned Rs 3000 a month and was happy because he enjoyed his work. A bit of an irony—we were both, in a sense, in the same sector yet held such different views.' The conversation seemed to reinforce what Madhavan believed—you don't need too much to be happy. In the months to come, the satisfaction from doing work that contributed positively to society would make him realize this over and over again. 'People who say the opportunity cost of switching careers is high are fooling themselves. You will always make enough money to cover a comfortable standard of living. You don't need luxurious holidays, several big cars and five-star meals—that doesn't make you happy,' he says.

He moved to New Delhi, where he and Madhukar set up Parliamentary Research Service, later renamed PRS Legislative Research, as part of Centre for Policy Research (CPR) in October 2005. Being incubated in CPR gave them credibility yet the freedom to work on their own terms. 'CPR does not have any ideology and it is important that we be seen as neutral so that all parties accept us,' he says. 'The incubation period in CPR provided an excellent base for our work, and we had the advantage of being in an intellectually interesting place.'

With an initial grant from Ford Foundation, Madhavan, Madhukar and two others began writing brief summaries of the bills scheduled for that winter session. The first brief they prepared in November 2005 was on the draft of the Right to Education (RTE) Act, which the human resource development ministry had posted online inviting comments. Once they finalized the summary, they posted and emailed it to each of the 790 Lok and Rajya Sabha MPs, and uploaded it on the PRS website. It is a procedure they follow to this day. The RTE Act was eventually passed in 2012 in a slightly different form. 'If you read the brief and the debates on the Act in Rajya Sabha and Lok Sabha, you will find that some points made are similar to the ones we raised,' Madhavan says.

While compiling reports, PRS only uses data that can be cited: government and quasi-government data, committee reports, court judgements, peer-reviewed papers. All data sources are cited in the research notes so that the reader can make his or her own judgement on its reliability and neutrality, the bedrock of their line of work. 'We also meet a number of stakeholders. The internal rule is that the researcher must meet at least two different persons or organizations of each stakeholder group before finishing the legislative brief. Of course, some of them may be pushing their agendas, so we don't cite them but we use these meetings to understand different perspectives,' he explains. The reports have their contact information, and the team makes presentations to individual MPs or their parties if asked to. 'We don't charge the MPs anything. All we take from them is the coffee and snacks they serve during the presentation,' he says.

PRS's next brief on the pension bill, which was finally passed in September 2013, went out in December 2005. 'Whether the MPs choose to read the report or not is up to them but essentially, we are providing them all the information they need to make the best possible decisions,' he says. The first person to call in December 2005 was an MP from a southern regional party, who wanted help with the demand for supplementary grants. Madhavan is careful to emphasize that the names of MPs and parties should not be published though he is forthcoming about who was quickest to respond. 'Nine years ago, I had never met an MP so I was surprised by their interest and hunger to learn. Not all of them are like that but a significant number are, and that's a start,' he says.

Over time, more MPs began noticing that an envelope with details on subjects they were to debate and deliberate on was landing on their desks every now and then. Madhavan and Madhukar met parliamentary party officers and leaders to tell them what they were doing. 'It was not difficult to get meetings with leaders because most parties were intrigued by our professional background. In the mid-2000s it was rare to see IIT- and IIM-educated guys just out of the corporate world asking for meetings with MPs without wanting favours,' he says. These meetings did a lot to establish PRS as a brand and once MPs started noticing the unbiased nature of their work, they became popular. Early in 2006, a major party's parliamentary officer asked for 140 sets of briefs on a range of issues for one of its meetings. 'We had two days to deliver the lot, and we did it,' says Madhavan. A few months later, a leader of the same party called out of the blue and asked them to prepare a presentation for its MPs on upcoming bills. During the budget session of 2006, from March to May, more parties started calling for help, and they knew their idea had clicked long before the end of the two-year window they had given themselves. PRS keeps track of which parties are contacting them, and ensures that it mirrors the composition of Parliament. 'The moment that changes—if there are more calls from one party, it will mean that we are not being viewed as neutral. We know that parties trust us for our impartiality and that is our biggest asset,' he says. To ensure that neutrality is not compromised, all legislative briefs go through a three-level process of vetting, which includes an external lawyer.

The rigid neutrality means getting funding is a challenge every year—they not only have to ensure that they get funds to keep the work going but also that the funding is from a body that will not ask them to compromise on impartiality. After seeing the results of its initial infusion, Ford Foundation gave PRS a $100,000 grant in the first year. Funding came from Google Foundation a few years ago. PRS requires about Rs 7 crore a year, most of which comes from Indian philanthropists, high-net-worth individuals in the banking sector, foundations and institutions. They've refused payment from MPs because they want their work to be available to all. PRS is careful to keep funders out of its day-to-day functioning to prevent any possibility of them trying to influence reports. 'We have some rules to insulate us from any such potential pressures,' he says. PRS doesn't get a majority of its funds from one source—in 2013, for instance, no single funder gave more than 15 per cent of the total amount. Funders do not know what PRS is writing and only get a report after publication. 'We make it clear to any funder that they do not get any direct benefit from funding us. It is a pure philanthropic activity in supporting public interest. We have refused to take funds from some senior industrialists who asked us whether we can write reports favourable to their industry,' says Madhavan. Similar rules are in place for board members and staff to safeguard objectivity and independence. The board comprises only independent members with no links to funders. 'Board members do not get remuneration or sitting fees. They are on the board purely because they believe in the mission of the company,' he says. The staff is drawn from diverse backgrounds—law, management, political science, sociology, economics, engineering, public policy—with degrees from premier institutions, work experience in leading companies and passion for public policy. 'All senior staff has significant financial opportunity cost in being in PRS; that is, if money was a consideration, there are better legitimate options for each one of us. There is no reason for anyone to compromise on core principles,' he says. He sets targets for everyone in the team, much like corporates do, and has rigorous evaluation processes.

From 2009, PRS started holding briefings for all MPs every Wednesday when Parliament is in session. The closed-door meetings are held from 9 a.m. to 10 a.m. and PRS invites an expert on a topical issue to make a presentation. This is followed by an interactive session with the twenty to thirty MPs who usually turn up. 'Of course, this may not translate into immediate action but that is not the intent,' he says. 'These briefings are more about creating awareness about key issues.'

In 2010, the Constitution Club initiated the Thursday Bill meetings with PRS as knowledge partner. Again, fifteen to twenty MPs from the pool of about eighty regulars turn up every week. 'Thursday meetings are more action-oriented in the sense that we are discussing bills pending in Parliament on which MPs have to take a call,' he says. Madhavan is aware that MPs consider other factors such as voter sentiment, constituency requirements and political ideology but is happy that they come to PRS for fact checks and data with which they can buttress their arguments. 'The indication that they find this useful is the fact that they voluntarily come for these meetings at 9 a.m.,' he says.

While it is difficult to prove a direct link between a briefing and any intervention, there is a paper trail in some instances. In the judicial standards bill, 2010, for instance, PRS pointed out that the penalty for frivolous complaints was much higher than that for similar offences in other laws, which could deter complaints. The standing committee cited PRS and recommended lower penalties, which was incorporated in the version passed by Lok Sabha in March 2012. A similar provision, recommendation and action occurred in the Lokpal bill.

It wasn't just MPs who showed interest in their work—a number of young people too began asking for internships at PRS, wanting to learn more about governance and policy issues. So about five years ago, PRS came up with the idea of a full-time fellowship for graduates under the age of twenty-five along the lines of internship programmes that political parties in the US have. The fellows are attached to an MP and do background research for him or her, but stay far from party work. 'The moment they are asked to do anything remotely political, we pull them out of there. The fellowship is to give young people an idea of what governance is,' says Madhavan.

In 2012, forty graduates worked with MPs, with both sides saying they gained from the experience. By 2014, the number of applicants for the fellowship had shot up to 1100, including one from the Andaman and Nicobar Islands. 'That application threw me. I never imagined that so many people from across the country would have heard of our work because we do not advertise offline,' he says. PRS depends solely on Facebook and Twitter to post updates, as well as on that good old medium—word of mouth. Forty-six graduates were finally chosen to intern with MPs in 2014. PRS has also created a free database of about 4000 state laws, since Parliamentary laws are easily available but those enacted by the thirty state legislatures are harder to find. It's still being updated and the idea is to make it easier to understand the laws governing each of our lives.

Four years ago, four volunteers from McKinsey, led by a senior partner, helped PRS formulate a strategy plan for growth in both depth of research and breadth of usage. PRS has started reorganizing its research teams to move beyond just lawmaking and help legislators ensure implementation and allocation of funds through the budget process.

Though PRS engages with about 400 MPs and 250 MLAs on a regular basis, it is trying to expand its reach. 'The goal is that more than half the number of MPs and 20 per cent of all MLAs should reach out to us whenever they look for credible research inputs,' says Madhavan. He says they haven't done as much as they should to get the public involved directly though they have been engaging with media and civil society groups to inform citizens about the work of legislatures. 'If you see a media article on Parliament with data, 70 per cent of the time, the source will be PRS,' he says.

Though Madhavan has a plan in place there are disappointments to face as he is an impartial professional dealing with a rather unprofessional class that has been accused of every sort of crime from skimming funds and possessing weapons to rape and murder.

'The way I deal with it is this: People have elected these MPs, and after they are elected, all of them have the same role to play as legislators. We at PRS are here to help them to play that role. In order to do our work, we are blind to "other activities" of MPs, and restrict ourselves to their role in Parliament,' he says, adding that other organizations are working on decriminalizing the system and PRS provides whatever support it can.

It isn't always possible to stick to this selective vision, especially when these 'other activities' hold up the working of Parliament, the institution they are trying to push along. The 15th Lok Sabha, for instance, stood out for a number of wrong reasons—it had a low number of working days, the largest percentage of time wasted due to disruptions, a low number of legislations enacted, and budgets passed without discussion.

'Yes, it really disappoints when Parliament doesn't function. Or it passes important legislation without due deliberation. Or when it fails to perform its accountability function,' he says, citing the example of the 2G spectrum allocation, which blew into a storm with allegations that the loss to the government totalled Rs 176 lakh crore.

The standing committee on IT looked at the spectrum issue in 2005 but failed to give a clear policy direction on the method of allocation. 'If it had done so, we would not have had the scam. Then the post facto scrutiny took place,' Madhavan explains.

The Public Accounts Committee examined the report by the Comptroller and Auditor General but was unable to submit a report. The Joint Parliamentary Committee gave a report, which was approved by the thirty-member committee in a 16–11 vote (three members were absent), and several dissenting notes were expunged by the chairman. 'In sum, we have closure from the JPC but no clarity. Parliament has failed, both to oversee policy, and as a fact-finding and accountability body,' he says. 'It is hard not to feel let down.'

That is when Madhavan reaches into his innate faith in democracy and the way it has worked in India (except for the brief blot of the 1975 Emergency) compared to other Asian and African nations that got independence around the same time. 'Parliament is the key institution—other than the higher courts—that can protect us from a potentially tyrannical government. We need to work on two tracks to make it better. One is to strengthen its processes and systems by supporting MPs; and two, is to inform the public and encourage higher engagement, so that the demand for performance from voters brings about improved functioning,' he says. 'We have to put our money where our mouth is.' To call him merely patriotic or optimistic is too simple. Madhavan is very aware of everything that is wrong with Indian democracy and the many failings in the way Parliament works, but rather than throw up his hands, he's looking for constructive ways to make it a more effective body. 'The thought that this is possible—and perhaps central—to India's experiment with democracy, and that I am fortunate to have the opportunity to participate in this process, is what keeps me going. There is a sense of honour in being able to contribute to the process of lawmaking.'

The other challenge is starting from scratch every time the government changes. 'We had built relationships with a lot of MPs and half of them lost the 2014 elections. So we had to start over but it was easier than the first time because we have built a reputation and we had word of mouth in our favour,' he says.

By the end of January 2013, PRS, which had grown to about twenty people, moved out of CPR and was instituted as a non-profit company, Institute for Policy Research Studies, under Section 25 of the Companies Act. Early in 2013, Madhukar moved out of an active role and on to its board of directors, headed by former ICICI chairman N. Vaghul. Madhavan's new office is on the top floor of a music school just off Deen Dayal Upadhyay Marg in New Delhi, and beautiful music filters up the stairwell all day. 'I had planned to be with PRS for just two years but I began enjoying it so much that I've stayed on,' Madhavan, who is its president, says. 'In Bank of America I was employee number 28,000-something. Here, I am creating something.'

MADHAVAN'S TIPS

1. It helps to have an overlap between the skill set of the old career and the new one. The skill set may be built on a passion or a hobby, but you must have skills and knowledge.
2. Always set targets. I see each MP as a client even though he does not pay. Unless he comes back, there is no point in doing what I do.
3. Be professional in every aspect even if you are doing what you love. What you do must be useful at a broader level whether you are running a for-profit or a non-profit organization. You must serve people.

A RACONTEUR'S TALE

Arvind Gupta

More than thirty years ago, when few schools cared about children understanding concepts and not just learning by rote, Arvind Gupta threw up a job as an engineer to make toys from trash—so that he could teach children to love science.

Arvind Gupta has got a truckload of new playthings. A friend sent him 600 CDs and plastic bottles, the detritus of an IT seminar, and he's spent the past week snipping, bending and glueing, doing what he does best—turning trash into toys.

He holds up a 200-ml Bisleri bottle with shiny discs implanted in its sides and a long metal rod skewering it. 'This is a great way to demonstrate the concept of a wind turbine,' he says as the contraption catches the fan's breeze and spins merrily, the sliced-up CDs reflecting light, rainbow colours bouncing off the floor of the large room stacked with books, toys, bits and bobs of all kinds. Every surface is covered with a toy or the promise of one.

An electrical engineer who started his career at Tata Motors, Arvind has spent the last thirty-five-odd years as a toy inventor. He makes science fun by doing experiments in schools and getting children to create their own toys to understand basic scientific principles. Reading and storytelling are his other passions so he writes books and translates hundreds of others into Hindi so that anyone can read stories such as Richard Bach's *Jonathan Livingston Seagull*, Art Spiegelman's *Maus*, and Isaac Asimov's *How We Found Out* series on scientific breakthroughs. 'Growing up, I didn't have access to many books. I don't want anyone else to be limited by that. Stories move people more than anything,' says Arvind, who heads the Children's Science Centre at the Inter-University Centre for Astronomy and Astrophysics (IUCAA) in Pune.

In a campus full of serious space scientists using laws of physics and chemistry to question the beginnings of the universe and understand our place in it, Arvind the inventor is a quirky and gentle soul who has spent his life teaching the basics of science and sharing his love for the subject so that children may one day debate bigger scientific questions. He describes himself as a Gandhian at heart, wears a kurta over trousers that flap an inch above his ankles, and derives simple joy from his own inventions and achievements that he hopes will spark the imagination of someone somewhere. He's a rambling raconteur who digresses easily into monologues on education, tales of nineteenth-century trade unionists, and anecdotes about famous friends.

His gravelly voice and precise diction seem to lend conviction to the way he speaks, and though he moves fairly slowly and deliberately, there's a sense of suppressed energy about him. He drops a thin black-and-yellow book on the table. *The Story of Solar Energy* is an illustrated biography of the sun, which Arvind wrote after the Fukushima nuclear disaster following the March 2011 tsunami in Japan. 'I was so angry and depressed by it. Then I felt I should channel that energy into something positive. So I wrote this. I thought people should know about how different cultures used the sun's energy in the past and how we can now,' he says.

Though he is best known as a toy inventor and is a popular science teacher, there is no limit to Arvind's curiosity. His website www.arvindguptatoys.com has more e-books than you can count, in English, Hindi, Marathi and other languages, on topics ranging from science, philosophy and education to architecture and astronomy, all for free download. There is a section on children's fiction, Russian classics and even inspirational books, which his team has uploaded after contacting publishers around the world for permission, then scanning page by page. 'We always have one volunteer scanning books. My motto is "A million books for a billion people". No one should be denied reading material,' he says, indicating a corner of the office where a student is assiduously turning pages into PDFs.

Arvind wanders barefoot around the 400-sq. ft room in IUCAA that he shares with three other scientists, the volunteer or intern of the moment, and piles of egg cartons, books, straws, magnets, rubber bands, flip-flops, floppy discs, CDs, and assorted rejectamenta. 'This is modern-day junk that we use. People give it to us and feel good about reusing and recycling and all that, but they do not consume less,' he says. Finished toys litter the shelves; half-finished ones wait for their creators to return; homemade pinwheels spin in the breeze; birds, houses and too-large insects fashioned from magazine covers are glued to monitors, and happy-looking skeletons cut out from paper flap on the walls of this toy factory like no other.

Twice a week, students from local schools come to the centre to watch the staff fashion toys from junk, play and make whatever they want. 'Children learn concepts from textbooks without understanding how they work practically. We try to bridge that gap by letting them have fun with science. In India, the commonality between a PhD and a primary school student is that neither ever gets hands dirty with practical science,' he says, setting a CD glued to a marble spinning on the cluttered table. 'See, a top. Once you make your own, you'll never forget that a good top has low moment of inertia and produces kinetic energy. Most simple toys are based on principles of physics. For hardly any money, a child has a toy and has learnt something,' he says.

This is the idea—simple and sensible science teaching— that drew Arvind away from the world of Tata trucks, a steady salary and corporate comfort at the age of twenty-five when his family thought he was nicely settled into a good job.

'I grew up in Bareilly in Uttar Pradesh, where my father was a failure of a businessman,' says Arvind, who was born in 1953. The family was always in debt but his mother was determined to send his two brothers, sister and him to school and so sold her jewellery to pay their fees. Arvind worked hard and ended up topping his district in the government intermediate examinations. He got a merit-cum-means scholarship to IIT Kanpur to study electrical engineering.

For a poor boy from a small town, IIT Kanpur offered all sorts of opportunities and exposure. 'IIT was heaven.

The library was fantastic, there was a film club, passionate teachers, an elite peer group, swanky infrastructure . . . I went crazy there. We saw the world's best cinema and listened to the country's best musicians. There was so much to tune your sensibilities,' he says.

Back then, IIT laid a lot of emphasis on social sciences so he took classes in philosophy, English, political science and economics along with his core subjects. The library was open from 8 a.m. to midnight every day and students could borrow ten books at a time. Arvind read everything he could lay his hands on.

The institute also had an aeromodelling and auto club but most of the students only flew the model planes and discarded them if they ran into trouble. He and his friend Akhilesh Agarwal fixed the broken engines and models and sold them back to the rich kids. 'I realized then that I'm a tinkerer at heart,' he says.

The 1970s were the years of student protests in Paris, the civil rights movement and anti-war protests in the US, the emergence of the environmental movement worldwide, and of Naxalism in India. World events trickled into the Kanpur campus and students spent hours discussing them. 'I found it a waste of time just to talk,' says Arvind. Instead of spending abstract hours discussing 'class conflict' and 'state hegemony', he and his friend Ashok Jhunjhunwala—now a professor at IIT Madras who works on taking technology to rural areas—decided to help the mess workers' children get an education. 'Here was a true example of class conflict. We studied in an elite institution yet the children of the workers who served us the chai over which we had these debates did not even have a school,' he says.

So they joined a group on campus, Sahyog, and went from door to door collecting money to begin classes. It was

Arvind's first experience of teaching. 'The class had about thirty students and I realized how eager children are to learn, how quick they are to pick up,' he says. He spent three years juggling college and teaching and saw the first batch finish their high school exams.

While he's chatting, his hands are busy. He saws through an old CD, sticks the triangle into the base of a discarded flip-flop, makes two deep incisions and inserts four ring magnets. He slips a couple more ring magnets on to a pencil and sets the pencil spinning, its nib against the cannibalized CD. It stays suspended in mid-air, held in space by the opposing forces of the sets of magnets. 'Magic?' He chuckles. 'This is the principle on which the Maglev [magnetic levitation] train runs. If a child assembles this for himself, he'll never forget and never want to give up science. It doesn't cost much for a school to buy a whole lot of ring magnets. The rest is all junk. Schools are mass factories that churn out idiots. Make learning related to life and it becomes more interesting,' he says.

One of the many speakers who came to IIT Kanpur in 1972 was Dr Anil Sadgopal, who was running the Hoshangabad Science Teaching Programme in sixteen government schools in Madhya Pradesh. Sadgopal wanted to improve science teaching using activities that could be put together with low-cost, locally available materials so that children in villages no longer needed to merely memorize definitions and formulae. The idea of simplifying science and the image of children busily doing experiments and loving them enchanted Arvind.

After college, he got a job at Telco—now Tata Motors— and moved to Pune for training in 1975. 'The campus was beautiful and the people friendly. I was in the maintenance division and enjoyed my work,' he says. About a year in, he began to feel that it wasn't for him, that something wasn't right. 'At that time we didn't have such words for it, but I was what is now described as "socially aware". My work did not fulfil that part of my mind. I just knew I was not born to make trucks,' he says. 'I didn't know what I wanted to do but it was enough to know what I did not want to do.'

Most of his peers—colleagues as well as former classmates—seemed perfectly content to have studied in the best institutes in the country and landed jobs in the best companies of the time. 'It wasn't enough for me, but I couldn't understand why,' he says. To work through the turmoil in his mind, he thought back to the days in IIT when he had felt happiest and most inspired. 'I remembered Dr Sadgopal's talk. Using so little to do so much, that was inspiring,' he says. Arvind wrote him a postcard asking if he could visit. 'That fifteen-day trip opened my eyes. I loved his stories of struggle and science.'

Back at work, he told his employers he wanted to join the science project and they gave him a year off. 'The 1970s were a time when everyone believed in going to the villages and starting there to bring about change,' he says.

In 1978, Arvind set off for Pallia Piparia village in Madhya Pradesh with his uncles' dire warnings of poverty and his mother's encouragement. 'My mother said, "Good, now you will do something useful with your life." My uncles said, "It is a mistake. Village life is not for you." I focused on the positive things my mother said and ignored the rest.' It's the approach he has taken most of his life—looking at the positives to overcome the negative.

In the first week, he went to the local market to see what he could find to work with, and bought one specimen of everything being sold on the roadside. Among the paraphernalia was a foot of bicycle valve tubing that cost 10p and a matchbox for 15p with which he started experimenting.

He cut the matchsticks and tube, balanced them, weighed them, filled them with water and sand, measured them, played around and pondered. He discovered that the drawer of the matchbox holds 20 ml of water—a handy bit of knowledge for village schools that cannot afford to buy glass measuring tubes. One day, while he was fiddling with the matchboxes and cycle tubing, a matchstick slipped snugly into a length of the black cycle tube. He picks up tubing and slides a matchstick in to demonstrate. 'Another matchstick went on the other end. I had made a flexible joint of two.' He wiggles the two matches to show how supple the joint is.

It was the beginning of the work that would make him famous as the master of Matchstick Mecanno and win him the Central Government's inaugural National Award for Science Popularization amongst Children in 1988. 'With these simple joints, you can demonstrate the properties of the acute angle, obtuse angle, right angle . . . Another bit of tube on the other end of the match and you can connect them to make a triangle,' he says.

Arvind speeds up, picking up a range of shapes he has already made and rattling off the properties of rectangles, rhombuses, squares, parallelograms, all the while pulling and pushing the jointed matchsticks to make different shapes. Suddenly, it's back to the triangle. 'See if you can push the triangle into some other shape. No? A triangle is solid, rigid. This is the basis of all civil and mechanical engineering: If you want stability divide a space into triangles; but so few engineering students appreciate this simple concept because they've never seen it practically.' He seems to be in showman mode as if he's giving a TED talk or holding a workshop, almost listening for the applause that his practical magic always draws. He demonstrates the making of a three- and a four-way joint and shows three-dimensional shapes. Despite the fact that you know what comes next, having seen the videos at least ten times on YouTube, you find yourself exclaiming with glee at the simplicity, the ingenuity, the sheer fun and his own enthusiasm for his matchless shapes. 'So simple, so simple. I love it. I'm hooked to these shapes and their science,' he says.

During his year off from Tata, he took the train to Trivandrum and spent four months working with his other college-day hero, architect Laurie Baker, who used local designs and materials to build houses for the poor. 'He was an amazing man, so full of fun and laughter yet doing serious work that touched others.'

Arvind went back to Tata early in 1980 after his year was up but couldn't settle in. He enjoyed the work since it involved tinkering with trucks but it didn't make him happy. Questions like 'Who does my work really benefit?' and 'Why do the people who work the hardest get paid the least?' kept eating at him.

When his mother fell ill, he quit and moved home to Bareilly to nurse her till her death at the end of 1980. 'It is one of the good things I have done in my life,' he says. 'She is the one who gave me very high self-esteem and self-worth, and the belief that you can't eat rupees and dollars because it is meaningful work that sustains you.'

From 1981 to 1983, he was part of an iron ore miners' trade union in Chhattisgarh, teaching the workers' children and editing the union's newspaper. 'I was full of idealism. I loved those days. I learnt how the other half lived and died. It lent meaning to words such as integrity, labour and equality that we'd grown up talking about but not really practising,' he says.

Around this time, his sister and brother-in-law placed matrimonial ads in newspapers for him. 'Sunita, now my wife, responded. She is wonderful, and came out to the mines for a year,' he says. 'I don't know anyone else who would have so willingly accepted someone like me, someone who wasn't ready to do what everyone else did.'

They returned to Pune in 1984, just before the birth of their daughter Dulari. 'We had no money, so we came back,' Arvind says. He applied for and got a grant from the Department of Science and Technology to write a book on his matchstick models, *Khel-Khel Mein*, which he later translated into English as *Matchstick Models and Other Science Experiments*. It has since gone into thirteen Indian languages and sold over half a million copies. Since then, he's written twenty books on simple science, and translated more than 160 into Hindi.

In the late 1980s, the family moved to New Delhi as Sunita wanted to do a PhD at Jawaharlal Nehru University. Arvind ran the science club at Mirambika Free Progress School, where his daughter studied, and conducted workshops. He started creating experiments for NCERT textbooks and joined the National Book Trust's advisory panel, and has continued with both for the past twenty years. He also did a series of programmes for Doordarshan, teaching children to make toys from trash. 'Children want to make things, do things, not just study the textbook,' he says. He conducted workshops in more than 2000 schools in India, and at seminars and conventions around the world.

Once Dulari went to medical college in Vellore, Arvind and Sunita decided to move back home to Pune in 2003.

Sunita got a job teaching sociology at Fergusson College. 'I'd always freelanced yet managed to do things I liked. I wasn't worried about starting over,' he says. 'For fourteen years, I cooked lunch and kept house for my wife and daughter. I did science workshops in all 300 schools in Delhi but I'd be home by 2 p.m. to give them food. Having the time to watch my daughter grow up and provide support while my wife studied and worked has been one of the good things of this career.'

Though Arvind hasn't been part of the mainstream, his IIT old-boy network has helped him. He often strays into stories of an old friend or a friend of a friend who helped out—friends who turn out to be captains of industry, respected educationists and activists, highly placed bureaucrats, or their friends and relatives. It is clear that the goodwill and respect he has is entirely due to the kind of work he does and the energy he brings to it. 'I have a very undemanding family and a groundswell of good feeling that keeps me going. My "wife insurance" is good, plus I am an eternal optimist,' he says, chuckling.

In October 2003, when IUCAA called him with a plan for a science centre funded by Tata Trust, he signed on happily. 'The four of us here work at a tenth of our market salaries because we believe we must do something worthwhile every minute of our lives,' he says.

Since 2009, when a friend taught the team how to use a video camera, record audio and edit films, they have been filming their experiments and uploading them on YouTube. The videos are no-nonsense affairs—a red cloth on a table serves as the set against which a pair of hands demonstrates the experiment while a clear voice-over explains the concept. The 4600 films have gone into eighteen languages and more than 50,000 children view them every day.

The videos and documents are free for anyone to translate as long as his team is credited.

Someone in Poland dubbed one of his films into Polish in August 2012. 'It was viewed five lakh times in a month. They wrote us a letter saying they had never seen anything like it. Neither had we, so we used Google translator to understand the letter,' he says, chuckling at one of his rare jokes.

Arvind retired from IUCAA at the end of December 2014, after he turned sixty-one, and now splits his time between Pune, where Sunita still has three years to go before retirement, and Vellore, where Dulari works as a paediatrician. 'In January 2012, I was diagnosed with prostate cancer and went through forty-two rounds of radiotherapy. I am fine and stable but I think it's time to focus on my other passion,' he says.

That 'other passion' is translating books into Hindi. 'When I was growing up, I always felt there was never enough to read in Hindi, the language I was most comfortable in. Maybe that's why I have 10,000 books now. Childhood deprivation leads you to swing to the other extreme,' he says. 'Until people read good books, how will they write them?' Arvind will continue to spread the good word by translating books into Hindi to add to the 170 digitized versions on his website. 'Everyone should have access to books,' he says. 'There is deep joy in sharing.'

ARVIND'S PLAY WAY

1. Play is serious business. Children—and adults—who play are happier people. Make your work your play.
2. Do something worthwhile with your life. Always ask questions of your life—if you are happy, if you are doing something meaningful, if this is what you were made for.
3. We have only one life and we must live our own dream, never a stale corporate dream.

TO THE BEAT OF A DIFFERENT DRUMMER

Raghu Dixit

Raghu Dixit threw up a career in microbiology to chase a dream of being a rock star and is now the frontman of a world music band, the Raghu Dixit Project.

On the faraway stage are little specks in motion carrying guitars. There are cheers as the crowd's hopes surge—the helpers are setting up. We're finally going to hear the music we have been waiting for, jabbing elbows in ribs and stepping on toes to make some space in the 35,000-strong crowd in Palace Grounds in Bangalore.

At last, some guys are stepping up to the mike. But wait, this isn't what we have spent more than two hours waiting for. We want Bryan Adams! These are khadi-clad reminders of the age of Doordarshan and classical music that we are desperately trying to forget while we wait to sing 'Best of me' and '18 'til I die' as we've seen thousands of delirious fans do on MTV. Instead—horror of horrors!—the Shankarabaranam raga breaks out. After a moment of silent disbelief, the crowd begins to boo.

'That went very well,' says contemporary folk and rock musician Raghu Dixit, remembering his first big gig as the opening act for Canadian rock star Bryan Adams in Bangalore on 4 May 2001. 'All we could hear was "We want Bryan, we want Bryan".'

When I tell him that I was in the ignorant crowd that booed, hissed and shouted obscenities at him from the cheap seats more than twelve years ago, his rich, rolling laugh fills the room. 'Ya, we rocked that crowd,' he says. 'But something good came of all that anger—35,000-odd people learnt the name "Antaragni",' he says, referring to his first band.

It is a combination of this obdurate, almost perverse optimism and a self-deprecating sense of humour that has helped former microbiologist Raghupathy Dixit plug away at his dream of being a rock star. Steady toil, dogged ambition and sharp business acumen have built his band, the Raghu Dixit Project, into one of the most sought-after performers on the indie music scene in India and abroad. That is quite a feat considering he sings in his mother tongue Kannada and in Hindi to crowds that, more often than not, have no clue what he's making a noise about, but are nonetheless moved by the large-heartedness of his music.

The music may be free-flowing and moving and the band members talented as numerous critics will tell you, but Raghu's worked hard to make a place for himself on the world stage by carefully structuring his band as a business and constructing its contemporary yet very Indian image.

Raghu is settled on a low black sofa in the living room of his flat in central Bangalore, wearing a pair of blue jeans and an old white T-shirt. Everything he's likely to need for the rest of the day—except lunch—is at arm's length. An acoustic guitar lies on the flat back of the sofa, a notebook, some papers and pen next to it, his phone is plugged in nearby, his laptop is beside him, and a jug of water and a steel tumbler sit on the floor. 'This corner is mine when I'm home. I do all my composing, business, calls, everything from here. I don't move,' he says, stretching one arm to pat the guitar, then the phone, and the other to the laptop.

He's rarely home to spend time with his wife, contemporary dancer Mayuri Upadhya, because the band is touring most of the year. They average 100 concerts a year in India, and spend at least three months in the UK, apart from travelling to festivals in other parts of the world. And there's one song that is always on his playlist whether he's performing at a TED talk in India, for a Dewarists TV show, in a stadium in Mexico or for the Queen of England— it's the first one he wrote, the ballad-like '*Mysuru se aayi*', a nod to his roots.

'It's a song that's very close to my heart because it keeps me in touch with where I came from,' says Raghu, who was born in Mysore in 1974 and lived there till he finished his master's degree in microbiology.

He grew up in a conservative Brahmin family that laid stress on discipline, academics and the classical arts, in that order. So there was no arguing when his father enrolled him in Bharatanatyam classes when Raghu was eight. 'I was the only boy among fifteen girls, but I was scared of him and didn't dare to bunk class,' he says. As time passed, he was noticed for his style and technical perfection. 'I love attention so I enjoyed the praise. I learnt dance passionately for seventeen years, till I moved to Bangalore to get a job when I was twenty-three.'

The dream was to be a professional dancer, but the reality was studying and getting a job. After finishing pre-university, he studied microbiology at Yuvaraja's College. With dance and academics taking up his life—'I was always in the top five in class'—music wasn't on the horizon, though his mother, a clerk in the postal department and a trained Carnatic music singer, would have the radio tuned to classical stations all day.

Oddly enough, it was Bharatanatyam that led him to the guitar. He gave a performance when he was in his second year of college, and got laughed at by his classmates. 'I think that's a running theme in my performances,' he says, his full-bellied laugh rolling out again. 'I was backstage removing my make-up when a classmate, Jeffrey, who played the guitar, walked in, and started taunting me for being effeminate and uncool. I was so angry,' says Raghu.

He challenged Jeffrey to learn a few steps in two months, in which time he'd learn to play a song on the guitar. 'Whenever I've been told I can't do something, I push myself to do more,' says Raghu.

He needed free lessons since the guitar was a forbidden, modern instrument in his traditional home, and he only wanted to learn one song. A friend named Leo introduced him to two priests in a local seminary. Amused by the young Raghu's obstinacy, Brother Peter and Brother Ivan showed him the basics and lent him a handbook and a guitar that he could play in the field behind the seminary. He spent a month practising his holds and mastering the handful of chords essential to complete a scale and eventually a song.

The only non-religious song the brothers knew was the semi-gospel, folk number '500 miles' by Peter, Paul and

Mary, about a pilgrim far from home and unable to find his way back. 'I was going to take on the coolest boy in college with a religious number. I didn't have a choice.'

The next month was one of discovery. For the first time, he was letting himself go. He felt pure joy at letting his voice travel any way he wanted and realizing that the song took on different meaning depending on the emotion he infused it with. Until then, even the arts had been restricted by rules of practice and tradition.

'I didn't know I could sing. I'd never heard my own voice before,' says Raghu. The challenge faded into the background, drowned by the discovery of his voice. The brothers taught him a few Konkani songs and Kannada ballads as well.

At the end of two months, it was time for the challenge. Jeffrey had forgotten about it so he had no dance steps but Raghu decided to sing anyway. A frisson of fear ran through him when he saw the crowd of students in the canteen. He'd only sung to empty fields.

'I closed my eyes and began to sing "500 miles". I got that feeling of being one with myself, of cutting off the rest of the world. It was surreal,' he says.

When the last line was finished, Raghu opened his eyes to a clapping crowd. 'They had genuinely enjoyed it,' he says. 'I felt something change within me. Here was something I did for myself yet it brought joy to others. Dance, as much as I loved it, had so many rules that it was only for others, not for me.'

He had discovered something he never wanted to let go of, but he had missed far too many classes and dance lessons to keep going back to the seminary. With a heavy heart, he returned the guitar and went back to his old life.

About a year later, a friend from Bangalore gave him a guitar as a gift, and Raghu spent hours hidden in the large garage behind his house practising. This was the early 1990s when Doordarshan began airing capsules of Grammy award shows, so Raghu listened to the era's hits— Phil Collins' 'Another day in paradise', Lionel Richie's 'Hello', Glen Medeiros's 'Nothing's gonna change my love for you' and artists such as Wham! and Michael Jackson. 'I loved them but there was no way I could record and learn them', he says.

So he just strummed and hummed along in the garage, and soon realized he was creating his own melodies. Newspaper headlines provided the first words for his tunes. 'I slowly understood how shorter and longer words work with the tune. Then I started writing my own words, and eventually my first full song, "*Mysuru se aayi*".'

He sang his songs a zillion times over so that he would not forget them. 'To this day, I can't read or write notations because I haven't learnt music formally. Now you can record a melody immediately on your phone or laptop and it will never get lost. I didn't have that luxury then, so I just sang and sang.'

College competitions followed and Raghu learnt to own the stage, winning most of the contests he participated in. 'That's how it went till MSc Music was a serious hobby, something I loved, not something I thought of as a career.'

During a college show in his first year of MSc, Raghu heard a classical Carnatic violinist named H.N. Bhaskar, and fell in love with his style. When Bhaskar's team was looking for a guitarist the next year, he signed up.

Bhaskar pointed out the Carnatic influences and ragas in Raghu's music, something he had not noticed before. 'I sang in English, but with Carnatic inflections. All those years of All India Radio playing at home, there was no escaping it,' he says.

They formed a duo, Antaragni, though they didn't have big plans for it—Raghu had to finish his MSc and get a job since his father had died and Bhaskar's parents made him move to Chennai to train under a violin *vidwan*. The two would jam when Bhaskar returned to Mysore on weekends. 'For me, it was pure joy. I didn't think about whether we were combining styles or doing something different,' says Raghu.

After he finished his MSc with a gold medal from the university in 1997, Raghu worked in the Central Food Technological Research Institute for a few months as a research assistant and moved to Bangalore to take a job as a college lecturer. About a year later, he joined pharmaceutical major SmithKline Beecham's data management department, doing research and documenting the results of clinical trials of vaccines. 'I had loved studying microbiology, but the passion for it was fading on the job,' says Raghu.

Life in Bangalore had its own rhythm—there were the working hours of a job that wasn't particularly exciting, the after-work hours of playing the guitar and singing at home and the weekends, which Raghu lived for. MTV was playing up desi pop, and the music scene was just opening up in the country. Bands mushroomed in Bangalore, many of them playing covers of popular hits, some being brazen and brave enough to perform their own material. Raghu was one of the foolhardy who went to the Sunday Jam sessions at Samsa open theatre behind Rabindra Kalakshetra with his guitar and memory full of melodies of his own making.

Sunday Jam, started by musicians Gopal and Geetha Navale in the 1990s, was something of a Bangalore institution, and one that helped now well-known performers such as Thermal and a Quarter, Raghu Dixit and Kryptos find their feet and an audience. On the first Sunday of every month, any band could go up and play for fifteen minutes. The audience—a motley crew of musicians, their friends and relatives, college students, music lovers and curious passers-by—would provide instant feedback in the most time-tested way: cheers or jeers.

Bhaskar and Raghu slowly won an audience among the Metallica and Eagles lovers. 'It was a fantastic concept. Even to this day, most big musicians from this city would thank Sunday Jam because it gave you a platform and an audience that was truly appreciative of anything new,' says Raghu. There were weekends when the boos were long and loud if the audience happened to mass towards the kind who judged music on the basis of how close it was to the original riff on a Guns N' Roses cover. 'If you didn't have a thick skin, you grew one,' says Raghu. 'You have to be ready for it if you're going on stage, actually if you're going to do anything that's not on the beaten path.'

Apart from the small but dedicated following, encouragement came from winning local contests. In 1998, Bhaskar and Raghu entered the annual music contest of National Law School, Bangalore. After the prelims, where each of the forty-six bands got ten minutes on stage, Bhaskar went back to Chennai. He was convinced that a classical violinist and an untrained singer whose English lyrics had a marked Carnatic touch would not get very far. Antaragni was among the six finalists and Bhaskar came straight back to practise for their twenty-minute slot. He won the Best Instrumentalist award, while Raghu was Best Vocalist. 'It gave me a lot of confidence,' says Raghu.

Work took priority though and in the middle of 1999, he was sent to the Belgium office for a training programme. They asked him to stay on after that month, which is when he began singing regularly in his room in a guest house in

Brussels to pass the hours after work. Fortunately for him, rather than evict him for disturbing the peace, the landlord liked what he heard and passed on a tape to a friend at a local radio station. 'Before I knew it, I had a small slot on the channel. I sang "*Mysuru se aayi*" and talked about myself a bit,' he says. The station head called him later to say listeners had been calling and emailing to find out more about him. 'He said, "If you can turn on an audience that does not understand the language, don't you think you can do much more in your own country?" It got me thinking,' says Raghu.

In ten days, he resigned, packed his bags and returned to India thinking 'I'm going to be a rock star'. 'I believed it completely. Till I was on the flight, I didn't think about what I'd done,' he says. He was twenty-four.

Back in Bangalore in early 2000, the starry-eyed Raghu found himself unemployed and quickly realized the rock-star business wasn't easy. 'I hadn't told my mother I had quit. I had to do something quickly because my savings would run out in a few months.'

While waiting for a concert of violinist L. Subramaniam and the German Philharmonic Orchestra to begin at Chowdiah Hall, Raghu got chatting with the woman sitting next to him. 'I told her what I had done,' he says. The woman ran a software company and needed technical writers. Raghu spent the next year and a half as a technical writer, typing up hundreds of documents and software manuals. 'It was boring but it paid the bills.' After work and on weekends, he would meet musicians and artists and perform with them.

That's when FM station Radio City announced a contest, and Raghu entered a song he, Bhaskar and another violinist had recorded. They won the Best Band award and got to play a live show in Palace Grounds with well-known rock band Pentagram and the other winner, Document Done.

'That was my first live concert, and the first time I played with a band complete with bassist and drummer,' says Raghu. In the audience was a scout from event management company DNA, but Raghu was more anxious about another person watching him: Mayuri, who he'd just met a few weeks ago. After the show, she said: 'Not bad.'

Mayuri may have feigned disinterest, but not DNA. They asked Antaragni to open for the 2001 Bryan Adams concert. Raghu's response: How much will you pay us? There was silence in the room. Indian bands were not expected to ask for money when they were being offered the prestigious platform of opening for an international star.

'I was adamant. If they thought we were good enough, why shouldn't they pay for our talent?' he reasons. 'Most bands don't ask for money because they think the exposure is worth forgoing the money, and event companies use that as a leverage point. Sometimes three or four opening acts will come and no one will get paid.'

Antaragni got Rs 60,000 and the performance led to a string of invitations to corporate shows, which earned about Rs 35,000 an appearance. After the Bryan Adams show, Raghu quit, traded in his employee stock options for about Rs 4.5 lakh, and bought himself a computer and a stack of books on recording music. He went back to Radio City and asked if they wanted any jingles. 'They said yes, so I started composing jingles at home and recording them.'

His first was for Spice Telecom—a mix of Kannada and English with the tag line 'Never miss an opportunity'. Raghu bursts into the peppy song, snapping his fingers to keep time, and then asks, 'Remember it? It was a super-duper hit on Radio City.'

Composing jingles and film music aren't just a way to pay the bills. Raghu considers them an opportunity to challenge himself creatively. 'The limits of timing, plot line, product pitch, they force you to try new things with your music. I enjoy it. Where is the joy without challenges?' says Raghu, who has composed songs for Kannada movies *Psycho*, *Just Math Mathalli* and *Kote*, and for Hindi film *Mujhse Fraaandship Karoge*.

'I don't have any qualms about the genre of music. I love metal, rock, Carnatic, folk, anything. Since I've never learnt music formally, I don't care about a jingle or a classical piece. My natural instinct is to sing, almost like a farmer in the field, free and simple,' he says.

To this day, Raghu's songs are simple things of joy. The tunes are not complex and his voice is usually the centrepiece of the arrangement with skilled instrumentalists providing additional layers. Raghu's entire song will have just two or three chords; a song with four chords would probably be considered complex. The lyrics are simple too—often just a few carefully crafted lines, repeated over and over, or the philosophical words of Kannada poets such as Shishunala Sharif.

Till 2008, Raghu wrote and composed jingles for a living because live shows didn't pay enough and Antaragni ran into the kind of crisis most bands do. Bhaskar found his Carnatic career taking off from 2003 and decided to drop out of Antaragni. Raghu tried continuing with the others, but the band wasn't holding together.

'We were not contributing equally and dreaming about the same thing,' says Raghu. 'Most Indian bands fail because they are not willing to work hard. They want the money and the fame but aren't willing to work for it. They think playing on stage for one and a half hours is work. That is the result. We rehearse eight hours a day. You are worth being on stage because of the work you have done before. I learnt discipline and commitment in the corporate world, but it's difficult to implement that in a band,' he says.

Raghu disbanded Antaragni in 2005, after which he spent time in Mumbai considering the possibilities of becoming a playback singer. He went to quite a few college music shows as a judge. 'You never know where you'll find talent. I would just jam with people and hit it off musically,' he says.

The impromptu sessions not only helped him recover from the band's break-up but also sparked another idea— an open house or laboratory for musicians that grew into the Raghu Dixit Project (TRDP) in 2007. 'I decided to let go of the idea of a fixed band and came up with a more fluid arrangement of collaborating with different musicians.'

Musicians can walk in and out as they please, working with him on just one song, or more if they feel they want to experiment and explore. They are paid for the work they do, rather than getting a share of profits as is customary for bands. The advantage is that musicians do not feel tied down and come without expectations. 'We enjoy the music, we learn from one another. We move on if we can't keep it up,' says Raghu.

The idea behind the music seems to be 'Let's just play it and have fun', an approach the entire band takes. They have great stage presence, and performances are happy, high-energy acts with musicians interacting and playing off one another, their bright lungis, kurtas and anklets adding colour to the stage. It's probably what makes his music so appealing to those around the world who have never even heard of a language called Kannada. 'I love the feeling of letting my voice out. Even today, that is the only reason why

I play music. It is a feeling I will not get from anything else,' he says.

It's also the reason why his album's credits feature names as varied as American clawhammer banjo player Abigail Washburn and Chennai-based percussionist Darbuka Siva. Over the last couple of years, bass guitarist Gaurav Vaz, flautist Parth, lead guitarist Vijay Joseph and drummer Wilfred Demoz have become regulars but they work with other musicians too. 'It is an unusual arrangement because most people see a band as one unit. We're like an ongoing experiment,' he says. 'We should both grow as musicians from the collaboration. Otherwise, there's no point,' he says, bringing up Gaurav, the band's manager and bassist as a case in point.

He spotted Gaurav playing Christmas carols at a coffee shop on Bangalore's Church Street in 2006. 'He wasn't a very good guitarist back then—he's excellent now—but I liked the way he moved with people,' says Raghu.

Bangalore boy Gaurav was a software engineer in Citrix, who had played in his college band and had seen Raghu perform at college shows. He loved coding and testing software, and played the guitar in the evenings. 'Music was something I enjoyed on the side,' says Gaurav, sipping a glass of strawberry-pink something in a restaurant off Brigade Road. 'Raghu asked me if I'd like to work with him and I said yes.'

Since Raghu was considering a few other guitarists as well—people who were on their way to making a name for themselves and not playing bass with just two fingers—Gaurav didn't think much would come of the offer, but he did start familiarizing himself with Raghu's music. 'I was used to listening to technically complex music. Raghu's music was very different and at first I didn't get it but I liked Raghu, so decided to work on it,' he says.

Gaurav would practise for two hours every morning before heading to work. Raghu did call, and was impressed with the then twenty-four-year-old's commitment to music he didn't fully understand. 'I wanted to work with good people, not just great musicians. Gaurav believed in me and my music from Day 1,' says Raghu.

It was a different line-up then. There was a tabla player, a flautist, Gaurav on bass, a lead guitarist and a classical percussionist or two. 'The music was similar to what it is now. Raghu's always had a plan for his music. I've grown to understand and appreciate his music fully,' says Gaurav, a bushy-bearded, lovable soul with varied interests and the ability to turn his hand to anything and become adept at it, whether it's growing plants with coconut husk as soil, playing the guitar, creating websites, or raising two cats with his wife Shilpa.

For a year and a half, Gaurav lived a triple life— rehearsals in the morning and work for the rest of the day, gigs on weekends in Bangalore, Mumbai and Hyderabad, and running his Internet radio station Radioverve. The band was getting busier and was being managed by Vijay Nair, who had also quit his job in a software company and started a music management company, Only Much Louder (OML).

In 2008, TRDP did a twenty-six-day Roots tour of the North-east. Time off from work was out of the question so Gaurav would work while they were travelling and between gigs and rehearsals. 'I felt sorry for him because it was a punishing schedule,' says Raghu. 'I asked him if he'd take a stake in the band and become my manager but he wasn't sure.'

Gaurav was also working with OML to set up its digital arm so that TRDP could get more visibility online. 'I worked closely with Vijay Nair and learnt the ropes of the music business. It was something that interested me,' says Gaurav.

The Roots tour changed Gaurav's outlook. 'Before our third gig, on the way to Itanagar, Raghu's car had an accident and he dislocated his shoulder. He still went on that night and played with as much energy and love as always. To see someone in that much pain give so much because he had committed to performing, that was a big moment for me,' says Gaurav.

After the Roots tour in 2008, TRDP was empanelled as an artist with the government's Indian Council for Cultural Relations, and did a five-country tour of south Asia, and appeared at the Rajasthan International Folk Festival. On tour in Asia—Singapore, Japan, Hong Kong, South Korea and Russia—Raghu realized, quite literally, that there was a whole world out there. If countries whose primary language was not English could relate so well to their music, they would probably have a bigger impact in the western world where they would be able to communicate easily with the audience. It was time to look west.

In 2009, OML got them a slot at the two-day Lovebox festival in London as well as a showcase spot in the Gibson showroom. 'I took a real chance. I knew we'd probably be on stage all of ten minutes for two performances, but I decided it was worth the risk and spent my money to get the band to London,' says Raghu.

They were a hit at Lovebox—where the headliners included Duran Duran—and have been going back every year since. In the audience at the Gibson guitar store was Paul Knowles of talent management agency Jenral Group. At the end of the show, he signed on to manage TRDP in the UK.

The experience changed the way Raghu looked at building his brand. The audience for his music was abroad, and courting that fan base was critical. He wanted to be a rock star, but that would happen only if more people all over the world heard him—and that wasn't happening.

Their first album, released by Hindi music composers Vishal–Shekar who had signed Raghu after hearing him perform at nightclub Zenzi in Mumbai in the mid-2000s, had been out for more than a year but hadn't made the impact Raghu wanted. OML's focus seemed to be moving to events, rather than managing bands, and Raghu felt TRDP needed more attention. There was more to be done but he couldn't do it all by himself.

Just when Raghu was casting about for new ideas to take control of the marketing, Gaurav found himself without a job. He'd taken a part-time job with a start-up so that he would have more time for music but the company never took off. Gaurav finally took up Raghu's offer to be his manager in December 2009.

The first year after Gaurav became TRDP's manager was spent consolidating what they'd built, and planning growth. 'Gaurav understands both the music and the business side and is fair, so people love to deal with him,' says Raghu. 'He's a large part of the reason we've been able to grow so much since 2010.'

In 2010, they played at the UK's WOMAD (World of Music, Arts and Dance) Festival, the biggest world music platform for international artists, and they've gone back every year since. 'The first WOMAD we played was a turning point for me,' says Raghu. 'We sold our CDs outside the venue, something we'd never done before. About 200 moved, the most we'd ever sold at one shot.'

That was also the year they appeared on *Later . . . with Jools Holland*, a contemporary music show on BBC2 that has about three million viewers in 100 countries. He was asked to perform 'No man will ever love you like I do' with two acoustic guitars, a violin and a tabla, not his ideal choice of song or instruments. 'But I went with it because the UK management was excited about it,' he says. That four-minute performance—on an hour-long show that also featured Robert Plant of Led Zeppelin fame, Mavis Staples, Fire and Adele—sent their album to number one on the iTunes world music charts. 'It was an amazing four minutes,' he says.

Raghu handles his band like a tightly run company, keeping track of expenses and incomes; living frugally like the CEO of a bootstrapping company without a salary or a car, still using autos to get around Bangalore. 'Everything I earn goes back into my music. If you have ideas of going abroad and performing and all that, it's a huge investment,' he says. 'It is very much like running a business. There is a huge amount of frustration and uncertainty. I get very angry when people call me lucky. It's been hard work. People feel jealous of me; it should be the other way around. I should feel jealous that they are living a comfortable life without worrying about where the money is coming from and where it is going.'

Raghu foots all the bills for three months of touring abroad—flight tickets for four musicians, hotel and food expenses and per diems. Add the costs of touring: hiring a van and equipment, paying for petrol, paying the tour manager, public relations agents, lawyer, TV and radio pluggers who help land spots for the band, the merchandisers, and it is, as Raghu puts it, 'an incredible investment'.

Invitations to festivals such as WOMAD and Larmer Tree (a five-day outdoor music and arts festival) do bring in money, but the expenses always race ahead. Raghu spends about £40,000 (about Rs 40 lakh) a year for the three months of touring, and for the past four years, the returns have been about £20,000 to £22,000 (between Rs 20 lakh and Rs 22 lakh).

'I fund it all myself in the hope of building a profile that will pay it back some day. To this day no Indian band has done what we have. That is what holds most Indian bands back—they don't want to put their own money out there to build themselves up,' he says. 'You have a good year and you create a cushion for a bad one, like any other traditional business.'

The year 2012 was 'terrible' for TRDP financially since many festivals had closed for lack of audience. Since it was an Olympics year, many people had spent their money on the games and had little left for music.

Musically though, it was a good year—TRDP performed for the Queen of England and the rest of the British royal family at her All the Queen's Horses show in May to mark her diamond jubilee. The year before, they played at the Glastonbury festival in the UK and won the SongLines award for Best Newcomer, one given by the world music magazine of the same name. 2013 was even better with the release of the new album *Jag Changa*, shows in the US and Mexico, more appearances in the UK, and a headliner spot at the NH7 Weekender in India.

'We are not yet a household name, and might never be. I'm spending so much money on building a career that is illusory. Some would say I'm mad, I say I love the music so it's worth it. I'll work out the business end soon,' he says.

It's the audience that he gauges his success by—hugs from fans, music lovers who travel from city to city to see him, groupies who bake brownies for the band to devour after shows, a French fan who sang 'No man . . .' Shah Rukh Khan-style in front of the Eiffel Tower and sent them the video. Raghu's even complied with requests made in advance to work 'No man . . .' into the playlist at a particular time in a show because a fan wanted to ask his girlfriend to marry him at the concert. 'It's people's love that keeps me going and gives me confidence,' he says.

The best compliment is when people walk up to him and say, 'We don't understand what you're singing but you're the happiest man on stage'.

'We don't sing in English yet people enjoy our music; that's a big achievement. We're a niche band and it'll take a few years of constant PR activity and performing to build a strong loyal fan base of 1000–1500,' he says. 'They are the ones who will create 10,000 fans for us.'

RAGHU'S NOTES ON LIFE

1. Everybody should do what they love. Eventually, you will be successful because you love it so much. I completely believe in that philosophy. I am a living example of it.
2. Playing on stage for one and a half hours is not work, it's the result of all the work you've put in to practise, get the gig and prepare for it. You are worth the price of admission because of the work you have done before. So prepare well for anything.
3. Whether you want to be successful in the music business, in a technology job or in the corporate world, you need discipline, commitment and the desire to push yourself to achieve more.

ACKNOWLEDGEMENTS

Most of the people without whom this book would not have been completed appear in its pages. They shared their stories with honesty and openness and patiently answered a number of questions that were, quite frankly, extraordinarily nosy. Some, I'm lucky to say, became friends along the way, the sorts of people you can't think of without a smile.

Thanks in particular, but in no particular order, to—

Murali Balan for sunshine.

Aparna Shekar Roy and Parvati Balchand Nanjappa for taking turns to be the cornerstone.

Paromita Pain for being an incomparably cretinous cretin.

Snigdha Manikavel who emailed suggestions, insights and photos of Mia throughout a Great Gatsby-like summer.

Charmaine Edwards for purple pens and pencilled-in corrections.

Susan Dileep for always bringing order where there is none.

Kuzhali Manikavel, Anoo Kulkarni, Arthi and Aditi Umachandran and Anjily Mahesh for steadfast support.

My employers, editors and colleagues at the *Times of India*. Jaideep Bose and Sunil Nair are exceptionally obstinate and encouraging editors.

Shekar Dattatri, Suprotim 'Picklu' Sengupta, Shilpa Krishnan, Dakshayani Kumaramangalam, Dnyanada and Sampada Chaudhari, Akshay Vishnu Madhavan, Preethi Sukumaran, Kamini Mathai and Phyllida Jay for advice and information.

Cibani Premkumar at Penguin for carefully going over every word.

And many, many thanks to Kamini Mahadevan, my endlessly patient editor at Penguin Books India without whom this book would not have been imagined.

Read more in Penguin

Subroto Bagchi

Zen Garden: Conversations with Pathmakers

For the immensely popular column 'Zen Garden', which he published in *Forbes India* for over three years, bestselling business author Subroto Bagchi spoke to some very interesting people. Many, though not all, of the visitors to 'Zen Garden' were, like Subroto himself, high-performance entrepreneurs. But the one thing that was common to every guest was that they were pathmakers—rather than choosing to follow the well-trodden path, they had charted new paths that others could tread on. This book features the very best conversations from 'Zen Garden', including those with the Dalai Lama, Sadhguru Jaggi Vasudev, Nandan Nilekani, Aamir Khan, Dr Devi Shetty, Kiran Mazumdar Shaw, Ekta Kapoor, social entrepreneur Harish Hande, Sanjeev Bikhchandani of Naukri. com, Deep Kalra of MakeMyTrip.com, Café Coffee Day's V.G. Siddhartha, Vikram Bakshi (the man who brought McDonald's to India) and India's top winemaker, Rajeev Samant. In their own words, these game changers reveal what it was that made them think differently, what gave them the courage to step off the beaten track, and how they sustained their vision in the face of seemingly insurmountable odds. *Zen Garden* is a book that every young Indian should read.

Read more in Penguin

Prakash Iyer

The Secret of Leadership: Stories to Awaken, Inspire and Unleash the Leader Within

Bestselling author Prakash Iyer uses simple but powerful anecdotes and parables from all over the world to demonstrate what makes for effective personal and professional leadership. Iyer draws lessons from sources as diverse as his driver, a mother giraffe, Abraham Lincoln and footballers in the UK. All of these stories come together in an explosive cocktail to unleash your inner leader.

The Habit of Winning: Stories to Inspire, Motivate and Unleash the Winner Within

Do you feel like throwing in the towel, but want to be a great leader? Would you like to build an organization? Do you want your child to be the best she can be? If you answered yes to any of these questions, *The Habit of Winning* is the book for you. It will change the way you think, work and live, with stories about self-belief and perseverance, leadership and teamwork. The stories in this book range from cola wars to cricketing heroes, from Michelle Obama's management techniques to Mahatma Gandhi's generosity. Together they create a heady mix that will make the winner inside you emerge and grow.

Read more in Penguin

Ankit Fadia

Faster: 100 Ways to Improve Your Digital Life

Our phones, computers and tablets are getting more powerful—
but how many of us know the ways to get the most out of them?
Bestselling author Ankit Fadia shows you how.

- Fake an incoming call on your mobile phone
- Catch a cheating partner red-handed
- Hide files inside photographs

Faster: 100 Ways to Improve Your Digital Life contains all the
tips and tricks for you to stretch the limits of emails, computers,
social networks, video sites and everything else digital. With
easy-to-use examples and loads of screenshots, *Faster* is the
perfect digital companion for you.

Social: 50 Ways to Improve Your Professional Life

This time Ankit Fadia expands his expertise beyond
computers and digital devices. He gives away technology tips
and general advice on useful apps that will help plan your
day, communicate effectively, build your personal brand and
manage your professional network. It tells you:

- How to do homework on people before you meet
  them
- How to get more work done on flights
- How to organize a PR campaign most effectively

Social puts you on the path of professional growth irrespective
of whether you are an entrepreneur or an industry professional.